DEFENSIVE TACTICS
FOR
SPECIAL OPERATIONS

SGT. JIM WAGNER

DEFENSIVE TACTICS
FOR
SPECIAL OPERATIONS

SGT. JIM WAGNER

Edited by Sarah Dzida, Raymond Horwitz,
Jeannine Santiago and Jon Sattler

Photography by Rick Hustead

Graphic Design by John Bodine

Models: Christopher Besse and Peter Falk

Library of Congress Control Number: 2007941016
ISBN-10: 0-89750-164-0
ISBN-13: 978-0-89750-164-4

First Printing 2008

BLACK BELT BOOKS
A Division of **OHARA** PUBLICATIONS, INC.
World Leader in Martial Arts Publications

ACKNOWLEDGMENTS

Regardless of how much talent or desire a person possesses, getting onto a special-operations team is in the hands of others. Fortunately, I know some good people who have either encouraged me, allowed me to prove myself, or took a chance on me as I moved in the direction of advanced tactics:

• Officer Dan Erber, my patrol partner with the Costa Mesa Police Department, who not only "watched my six" on many calls but also got me interested in sniper tactics and encouraged me to join the SWAT team;

• Lt. John Fitzpatrick, my supervisor with the Costa Mesa Police Department, who gave me my first big break by putting me right in the middle of the action doing tactical diagrams during a barricaded suspect call, even though I was only a patrol officer at the time;

• Lt. Ron Smith, the SWAT commander of the Costa Mesa Police Department, who authorized my placement on the SWAT team and authorized me to train with the U.S. Marine Corps, U.S. Army Special Forces and U.S. Marshals Service Special Operations Group on SWAT time, which helped make me the most crossed-trained officer on the team and utilized many of my talents in a variety of missions;

• Sgt. Darrel Freeman, my SWAT logistics supervisor at the Costa Mesa Police Department and eventually my field supervisor for patrol, who constantly encouraged me to keep learning all I could and to ignore those who were critical of progress;

• Sgt. Wilfred Moreno, my direct supervisor at the Orange County Sheriff's Department when I "moved up," who immediately saw my potential, promoted me to the rank of sergeant, appointed me as the Dignitary Protection Unit team leader, and rewarded me two years later by assigning me to an event in 2002 with President George W. Bush;

• Cpt. John Hensley, the commander of the Dignitary Protection Unit, who basically handed me the reins and let me train the 10-man unit as I saw fit, a position I took advantage of by bringing in German and Israeli counterterrorist instructors to augment the team's training;

• Lt. Bob McKean, my supervisor during my transition period with the Phoenix Police Department in Oregon, who placed me on the department's tactical team from day one and made me a defensive-tactics and firearms instructor;

• Maj. Frank Naumann, my current unit commander of the California State Military Reserve, 40th Infantry Division (Support), Provost Marshal's Office, who genuinely puts his men and women first and places more importance on skills than rank;

- Sgt. 1st Class Dennis Barberic, my direct supervisor at the Provost Marshal's Office who is a rare breed and who believes one cannot get enough realistic training;

- And to the men and women who selected and trained me on one of America's original counterterrorist teams—the Federal Air Marshal Service. I did 146 counterterrorist missions for them—what a rush!

I also want to thank the hundreds of police, corrections, probation and military personnel I have trained while I was an instructor of entry-team tactics, sniper tactics, firearms, special operations and defensive-tactics courses (patrol, institutional, investigative and SWAT). Teaching is a two-way street, and many of the people I have trained have shared their knowledge with me, leading me to compile some of the most effective techniques and training methods in the world.

Photo courtesy of Jim Wagner

Jim Wagner dressed as an Iraqi insurgent in 2006 while training the soldiers of the 40th Military Police Company, which earned him the California Commendation Medal.

DEDICATION

I dedicate this book to every law-enforcement, corrections, probation and military defensive-tactics instructor who strives to give their students the most realistic training they can in order to promote genuine safety.

Jim Wagner trained Germany's top counterterrorist team, the GSG9, in 1999 and 2000. This led him to train several German agencies and the *Ausbildungszentrum Spezielle Operationen* (German Special Forces).

Photo courtesy of Jim Wagner

SPECIAL THANKS

I would like to thank Christophe Besse, the director of my Reality-Based Personal Protection program in France, and Peter Falk, the director of my Reality-Based Personal Protection program in Sweden, for flying out to Los Angeles to appear in the photo shoot for this book. I would also like to thank the Baker Batshield company for supplying the revolutionary ballistic shield used in the photo shoot and Constable Garth Hoffman of the Delta Police Department in Canada for training me in this piece of equipment.

Jim Wagner

Jim Wagner on the January 2002 issue of *Black Belt*.

FOREWORD

In 1984, I read a book titled *The War Against the Terrorists* by Gayle Rivers, and I was fascinated not only by the various terrorist organizations wreaking havoc around the world but also by the counterterrorist teams that were tasked to confront them. Even though I was already a martial artist with a heightened awareness of fighting systems more advanced than the ones I had originally studied, I was still awed by the team's weapons, their high-tech equipment, and the pure intensity of the conflicts they faced between "good and evil." I had yet to be in law enforcement at the time, but from then on, I made a point of getting my hands on other books that dealt with counterterrorism and special-operations teams.

Just before Christmas 1988, I received my first official training in law-enforcement defensive tactics when I was hired by the Costa Mesa Police Department in Orange County, CA. As a corrections officer, I processed and housed prisoners in the jail. I also learned more about the criminal mind, which gave me a new perspective on conflict. I needed it because my traditional-based martial arts training hadn't prepared me for the brutality exhibited by many of the inmates I had to control and, on occasion, fight. However, after two years of working in the jail system, I wanted to broaden my experience with more training—and I also felt like I was "doing time." This is why I decided to apply as a police recruit, which I became after a lengthy selection process.

As a recruit, my police department sent me to the Orange County Sheriff's Training Academy in Garden Grove, CA—one of only six "stress academies" left in California at the time. Run in much the same way as a military boot camp, a stress academy includes lots of yelling, degradation, tearing down of recruits, full-contact matches and mental stress. In other words, perform well or lose your career. Yet in June 1991, I managed to graduate from the stress academy, and after training with three assigned field-training officers in the Field Training Program, I was finally cut loose to handle police calls on my own in Costa Mesa, CA. With a population of 100,000 at the time, Costa Mesa was a city with a mix of activity: gangs on the south side, richer areas to the north, industrial sections to the east and west, and a lot of retail outlets and residential neighborhoods in between. To handle that mix, the city's 175 sworn officers had it all: patrol, traffic, investigations, K-9, special-enforcement detail, gang detail, DARE, bicycle patrol, aviation and SWAT; basically, we had every team and unit a department could possibly desire.

In my case, ever since my first days in the police academy, I wanted to be on a SWAT team. However, because most members stay on a team from anywhere to five to 10 years, openings were always rare. Vacancies for the Costa Mesa SWAT team appeared after I had spent a couple of years as a regular police officer. As soon as the opportunity came, I applied—but so did a dozen other guys. I remember my tryout vividly because it was also the day of my 30th birthday, and my wife had planned a party to celebrate it at the Academy of Fighting Arts, the martial arts school I owned and operated on the side.

My test was on a sizzling-hot, breezeless, July day that began long after the coolness of the morning disappeared. Nonetheless, I was energized and ready to ace everything. I did 10 pull-ups on the chin-up bar. I dragged the 170-pound dummy 40 feet. I did 60 push-ups and then immediately rolled over to do 60 sit-ups to receive the maximum amount of points. I ran around the one-minute-or-less obstacle course, leaping the walls like a gazelle and weaving around the pylons like a slalom skier. I also had to run up a three-story flight of stairs within 15 seconds and ring a bell mounted at the top of the banister. Then, to finish the testing, I had to run a mile and a half on the scorching, hot rubber track. I hate long-distance running. I hated running in the Army, I hated it in the academy and I dreaded running, especially the timed runs, on the day of the SWAT test. But for this test, I ran my heart out only to discover that I had finished 40 seconds too slow. "Sorry, you didn't make it," the unemotional examiner said. I nodded in acknowledgment and found a bench in the shade to sit and let the heat slowly dissipate from my body. (Fortunately, my birthday party helped lift my spirits later that night.)

I was discouraged but not defeated, which meant that when the SWAT team had two new openings the following year, I applied. This time, however, I managed to kick it into high gear and cross the finish line under the allotted time for the mile-and-a-half run. I also passed the shooting test, which involves a hostage situation that uses projected images on a live-fire screen, and endured the oral board. The SWAT oral examination board is like a gladiatorial coliseum. Once the candidate has answered dozens of questions and left the room, the current SWAT team members and commander vote for the hopeful by giving them a thumbs up or a thumbs down. A few weeks later, I learned that the verdict had been in my favor when Lt. Ron Smith handed me a silver-plated SWAT badge for my patrol uniform. All he did was welcome me to the team and hand me my equipment list, but that day my emotions ran high.

During my time on the Costa Mesa SWAT team, I did a lot of outside training with the U.S. Marines at Camp Pendleton in California, which included Military Operations Urban Terrain training, helicopter rope-suspension training, range safety-officer training, and scout/sniper training with members of the 1st Marine Division Sniper School, who lived and breathed the motto: "One Shot, One Kill." Eventually, the Marines got wind of the fact that I was a defensive-tactics instructor, and before I knew it, I was training their Provost Marshal's Office, Special Response Team and other Marine units. I eventually began training the Department of Defense Police, the U.S. Navy Provost Marshal's Office, the Los Angeles School Police SWAT team and other agencies on the West Coast. As a direct result of this outside training and teaching, I—along with three of my cop buddies—formed an organization for the sole purpose of training law-enforcement, corrections, probation and military personnel. At first, we just provided sniper training, but later we expanded into entry-team training, and soon after, I created a defensive-tactics program.

Within a 10-year period, I had trained special-operations teams around the world in my ever-evolving special-operations defensive-tactics program. Some units that have requested my services include:

- British Columbia Sheriff's Department (Canada)
- California Department of Corrections SRT
- Diplomatic Protective Services (Spain)
- Escambia Sheriff's Department SWAT (Florida)
- FBI SWAT
- Grupo de Ações Táticas Especiais (Brazil)

- Grupo de Operaciones Especiales (Argentina)
- GSG9 Counterterrorist Team (Germany)
- Israeli Special Forces
- Lake County Sheriff's Department SWAT (Indiana)
- London Metropolitan Police Territorial Support Group
- Los Angeles Airport Police
- Los Angeles County Probation Department
- North Miami SWAT (Florida)
- Rosarito Grupo de Operaciones Especiales (Mexico)
- San Diego Sheriff's Department Prisoner Transport Unit
- Skagit County Sheriff's Department Cell Extraction Team (Washington)
- U.S. Air Force Security Forces
- U.S. Army Military Police SWAT
- U.S. Border Patrol
- U.S. Coast Guard Boarding Teams and Sea Marshals
- U.S. Drug Enforcement Administration
- U.S. Marshals Service Special Operations Group and Fugitive Task Forces (San Diego, Dallas, Washington, D.C.)
- U.S. Probation Office
- Vancouver Police SWAT (Oregon)

In 1999, I left SWAT and joined the Orange County Sheriff's Department, which is America's fifth-largest sheriff's department. Before I was even sworn in as a sheriff, I was approached by my supervisor-to-be, Sgt. Wilfred Moreno, who had seen my personnel package.

"You want to be on our new Dignitary Protection Unit, don't you?" Because he said this in a you-had-better-volunteer voice, I agreed. A few weeks later, the DPU was formed per the orders of Sheriff Michael Carona, and I was promoted to the rank of sergeant and team leader. This elite team was tasked with protecting celebrities, diplomats and Carona himself. Of course, I was put in charge of training the team, which naturally included a rather intensive defensive-tactics program that I created specifically for bodyguards. However, I was unaware of how important these skills would soon be in protection agencies around the world.

On September 11, 2001, terrorists attacked the United States, and the very next day I was assigned to anti-terrorism duties by my department. My first assignment was to run the main checkpoint for John Wayne Airport in Orange County because I was one of the few law-enforcement officers in my region who had been trained to identify Arab terrorists. I was also familiar with current terrorist tactics because of a recent training trip in Israel. However, as exciting as I found anti-terrorism, I was not content with my role because I had always been interested in counterterrorism. While *anti-terrorism* is about the prevention of terrorist attacks, *counterterrorism* is about hunting down and/or confronting terrorists. As a SWAT defensive-tactics instructor, I had trained with a few top-notch counterterrorist teams around the world, but now I wanted to be on the front lines in the "War on Terror."

In the end, I got my big break when the U.S. government scoured the country for anyone with special-operations training. I submitted an application and was selected as an agent for the Federal Air Marshal Service. At the time of my hiring, only three authentic counterterrorist teams existed in the country: the U.S. Marshals Special Service Operations Group, the FBI's Hostage Rescue Team and the Federal Air Marshal Service. Of course, there were the Special Forces, which dealt with international terrorism, but they operated outside the country, and it seems to me as if every major department has since created its own "counterterrorist team" because of September 11.

When I became a counterterrorist agent, the U.S. government flew me to the Federal Aviation Administration's headquarters in New Jersey for my initial training. I then traveled to the middle of the desert for my primary training at the Federal Law Enforcement Training Center in Artesia, NM., which ended with counterterrorism school. Besides weapons training, surveillance techniques and explosives training, one of my favorite courses was defensive tactics. I believed that my instructors were "squared away" and that the defensive-tactics program was realistic because we fought with training knives and guns, and engaged in full-contact combat while wearing protective body armor. I felt right at home in this class.

Upon my graduation, I was officially a part of Operation Enduring Freedom and assigned to the Los Angeles Field Office, which operated mostly out of Los Angeles International Airport. I had finally reached the top of the counterterrorism food chain and I loved every minute of it. Finally, I was living the life I had read about in that paperback book back in 1984. I had reached that dream.

As a federal air marshal, I participated in 146 counterterrorist missions, doing everything from surveillance of our nation's airports to finding weaknesses in the aviation security system to flying to unknown points with all the major American carriers. On two occasions, I did counter-surveillance on suspected terrorists, and I even had my team yank a suspect off a fully loaded passenger aircraft bound for Washington, D.C., which may have been because of the nuclear information I had found in his briefcase.

However, once it was obvious that the major threat of terrorism to the aviation industry was over, I decided to move on and resigned from the Federal Air Marshal Service. The decision was not hard for me to make. I had been writing my monthly column, High Risk, for *Black Belt* since 1998, and my reality-based defensive-tactics concepts were popular with readers because of their realism. I had a choice to make: continue working in counterterrorism as a "gray man" or promote my self-defense system, which was emerging on the scene in the United States and Europe. I decided to do the latter. Free to once again have my image published, I arranged with *Black Belt* to do my first DVD series titled *Jim Wagner's Reality-Based Personal Protection,* and my book *Reality-Based Personal Protection* soon followed. Although all eight DVD covers feature me in SWAT gear, the series is actually about teaching civilians how to protect themselves in modern criminal and terrorist situations. However, the series remains popular with police and military personnel.

After my stint with the Federal Air Marshal Service, I went back to teaching defensive tactics for special operations. I trained once again with the Israelis, I taught at the Oklahoma City Police Academy, I worked with maritime units in Florida and I trained the British for a third time in London. Without volunteering for it, my current agency made me a defensive-tactics instructor, which meant that along with carrying out my missions, I would also be teaching.

January 21, 2003, marked the day I officially began teaching the Reality-Based Personal Protection system, which contains a law-enforcement version that includes defensive tactics for special operations and a civilian version that meets their specific needs.

I wrote this book to give people a good look at a solid special-operations defensive-tactics program—one that has been 14 years in the making. The techniques and training methods found in these pages are based on my own involvement with elite teams around the world. They are "street tested," and they fall within any department's use-of-force policies. Many defensive-tactics instructors take traditional-based martial arts, throw a SWAT uniform over it and call it "Defensive Tactics" for SWAT, Emergency Rescue Team, Human Rescue Team, etc. Not so with this system. The Reality-Based Personal Protection system for special operations is just that—reality-based.

Photo courtesy of Jim Wagner

Jim Wagner was a team leader for the Dignitary Protection Unit of the Orange County Sheriff's Department from 2000 to 2002.

COMANDO DA AERONÁUTICA
QUINTO COMANDO AÉREO REGIONAL
BATALHÃO DE INFANTARIA

(TRANSLATION)

Letter # 001/BINFA/200   Canoas, September 19 th, 2000.

Dear Sir,

  This letter is to express our gratitude to Sergeant Jim Wagner, for training security members of Grupo Especial de Polícia da Aeronáutica – GEPA (Air Police Special Group), which is part of 15 th Security Police Battalion of the Brazilian Air Force, on this base at Canoas, Brazil.
2. His expertise in passenger aircraft assaults has contributed to a better trainning program for this unit.

     Sincerely,

     JOÃO **RAFAEL** MALLORCA NATAL, Major
     Commander, 15 th S.P. Battallion

To
Sheriff Mike Corona
Orange County Sheriff's Departament
California, U.S.A.

This is a letter of appreciation from the Brazilian Air Force, which later made Jim Wagner an honorary member.

TABLE OF CONTENTS

CHAPTER 1

ARM AND LEG STRIKES

Although special-operations personnel, or "operators" as they are properly called, are armed to the teeth upon entering a building or taking down a vehicle at a high-risk stop, most combative situations require empty-hand techniques rather than firearms. Less-than-lethal devices such as pepper spray and Taser guns are also great tools for subduing subjects, but an operator might not always have immediate access to these tools in a confined space or when a "cooperative" suspect suddenly goes ballistic. Therefore, it is essential that all members of an entry team be well trained in defensive arm and leg strikes, especially those unique to tactical situations. Notice that I apply the term "arm strike" rather than "punching" because of its greater versatility of meaning. In narrow terms of legal applications and the use-of-force continuum (See Appendix 1.), the word "punch" solely means striking someone with a closed fist, while an "arm strike" encompasses pushes, grabs, open-hand techniques and closed-fist attacks. They may also refer to single-hand strikes, elbow impacts if the primary hand is controlling a firearm, or both hands if the weapon is holstered or slung behind the operator, such as in the case of a submachine gun or an assault rifle. Kicks, meanwhile, are very helpful to operators whether they are in full combat glide, in the middle of a weapon transition or about to stop a charging enemy. Kicks are also powerful enough to provide "stopping power" if the operator targets a hostile subject's pelvic area. In fact, by launching a well-delivered forward thrust kick, I have been able to stop an aggressive adversary from inflicting any damage on myself or others.

In the Reality-Based Personal Protection system, there are a diverse amount of defensive arm strikes and kicks as well as proper stances for a variety of conflict-oriented situations faced by special operators. Yet at the same time, the system has a limited number of strikes to deal with an unlimited number of situations. Unlike other martial arts that have too many techniques to deal with one kind of attack, the Reality-Based Personal Protection system simplifies all categories down to 10 strikes each, thus making them more straightforward as compared to other defensive systems. This is because there are only five planes that each comprise two distinct directions that make the 10 primary ways to strike at or block a hostile subject. The forward and backward plane make up two directions (1, 2), while the horizontal plane consists of the directions left and right (3, 4). The vertical plane encompasses the directions up and down (5, 6), while the two diagonal directions make a letter "X" and include two downward (7, 8) and upward angles (9, 10). However, it should be noted that no matter the attack an operator faces, any search or arrest is made more safely with the aid of a cover officer or teammate to help control the situation.

CONFLICT STANCES

Because they are highly mobile, comfortable and practical, the Reality-Based Personal Protection system uses the same basic conflict stances as Roman legionnaires, Greek hoplites, Apache warriors or instructors in the Marine Corps Martial Arts Program. All strikes and kicks are launched from these positions.

ALERT CONFLICT STANCE

Dressed in operator's gear, Jim Wagner demonstrates that he is ready for possible conflict by carrying a long gun and adopting the alert conflict stance. His weapon blades his body with the primary side (weapon side) back.

In order to distribute his weight equally, Wagner places his feet directly under his shoulders, with one foot in front and the other one in the rear. The front leg and its complementary hand are known as the "lead," while the back leg and its hand are known as the "rear."

Even though a secondary weapon (the pistol) has replaced the primary weapon (the long rifle), Wagner tucks his weapon close to his body and scans the area for possible dangers.

When switching from a primary weapon to a secondary weapon or bare hands, Wagner transitions his rifle behind his back so it is still within easy reach.

ALERT KNEELING CONFLICT STANCE

In an open-area conflict, the operator reduces his profile by taking cover behind a barricade or crouching to the ground with his weapon.

Because operators face conflicts that may erupt anytime and anywhere, they are equipped with insert kneepads to prevent injuries when kneeling.

IMMINENT CONLICT STANCE

An operator faces an attacker, but his stance and weapon show he is prepared to meet the situation head-on. However, only the operator can decide what constitutes the appropriate amount of force in any given situation.

The operator holds a cornered attacker at gunpoint but remains alert to his movements. Even if your adversary's proximity is farther than shown above, it is important to approach any potential hostile subject with the attitude that conflict is imminent.

COMBAT GLIDE

Martial artists tend to posture for a fight, but operators are usually on the move. This is why this special glide is the launching pad for most kicks. It will also be discussed in more detail later in this chapter. (See page 41.)

Jim Wagner's U.S. Coast Guard students at the Port of Los Angeles learn how to combat glide.

Photo courtesy of Jim Wagner

A combat glide is used in a "stack" to move operators to the target more smoothly.

Photo courtesy of Jim Wagner

MAKING A CLOSED FIST

While many people are "all talk" when it comes to fighting, the defensive-tactics business has taught me not to take anything for granted, especially the simple stuff. This is why I'll go through the Reality-Based Personal Protection basics step by step in order to help people who aren't sure how to make a closed fist for striking.

Hold your hand straight up, keeping it free and clear of any objects. If you wear gloves while doing missions, also train with gloves on in order to simulate your reality.

Roll your fingers into a tight palm and wrap the thumb over the index and middle finger until the whole hand is like a hard ball.

The striking impact area of the closed fist is the index and middle fingers' knuckles. When aligned, these two bones line up with the bones in the arm and put more force into the impact.

For the first strike, hit your target in a straight line, then pull the fist back along the same line. This is known as the "piston concept" because the fist must penetrate the target and quickly retract like a piston.

CLOSED-FIST STRIKES

Over the past decade, defensive-tactics instructors have tended to promote open-hand strikes over closed because the chance of self-injury does not seem as great. In real-life special-operations conflicts, however, open-hand strikes do have their place, but not when it comes to the operator's own protection. This is because a closed fist is not only a natural instinct for most men, but the hard bone tissue of the knuckles also means that an operator with a hand injury won't notice the pain until he is in a safe area and at a safe distance from the original conflict.

FORWARD CLOSED-FIST STRIKE

Jim Wagner uses a closed fist to strike an attacker with his rear hand. Whether his rear defense comes from the right or left hand, Wagner must also rotate his hips in the same direction as his strike's target for power.

REAR STRIKE

After sneaking up behind Jim Wagner, a hostile subject is caught off-guard with a full swing rearward. Striking with his lead fist, forearm or elbow, Wagner follows through the entire hit, pivoting on his rear leg, before turning to face the man in a fight.

RIGHT HORIZONTAL STRIKE

The rear hand strikes forward from the rear side of the body traveling in a horizontal line until it hits its adversary. In this picture, Jim Wagner is in a left lead stance, but he can also strike from a right lead stance.

LEFT HORIZONTAL STRIKE

Similar to the right horizontal strike in that it also follows a horizontal trajectory, the left lead hand initiates this strike instead. The operator must pivot and roll his hips in order to follow through with the attack against his adversary. A lead right-handed horizontal strike also works.

VERTICAL UP STRIKE

The upward strike shoots straight up into the hostile subject and then quickly retracts. When executing this strike, Jim Wagner keeps his wrist and arm perfectly straight to avoid self-injury.

VERTICAL DOWN STRIKE

Using a hammerfist, Jim Wagner drops his weight down on his adversary's head. If the enemy is even lower to the ground than shown in the picture, an operator can strike him with his knuckles.

DIAGONAL STRIKE (RIGHT and DOWN)

In a diagonal strike, the operator brings his elbow up but strikes with a downward-slanting motion. In essence, his punch creates a diagonal line that can be traced from starting to impact point. In a right-and-down strike, the operator uses his right hand to attack by bringing his closed fist up and striking it downward to the left.

DIAGONAL STRIKE (LEFT and DOWN)

This time, the operator drives his closed fist into the attacker by following the diagonal plane from upward left to downward right.

DIAGONAL STRIKE (RIGHT and UP)

In this strike, the operator still hits in a diagonal plane but from down to up, right to left. Because it is an upward strike, he must rotate his body for extra power. Shown here: The operator attacks with his rear right hand.

DIAGONAL STRIKE (LEFT and UP)

The motion of a diagonal strike forces the attacker to lose his balance. This upward strike launches from left to right and down to up. Make sure that the wrist and arm are always lined up in any strike to avoid self-injury.

Jim Wagner (far right) watches his students during a full-contact scenario. The corrections officer makes contact with the SWAT officer with a horizontal strike.

Photo courtesy of Jim Wagner

WEAKER SUBJECT SUBMISSION STRIKES

In a law-enforcement or special-operations situation, slugging the face of a hostile subject who is not a true threat to the operator, such as an uncoordinated drunk or a slightly out-of-control teenager, can be considered police brutality. Therefore, these open-hand techniques, which I originally learned from the Israeli police, can help a person not cross the line into excessive force. The main distinction between these attacks is that they are legally defined as "slaps" rather than "strikes." A "slap" is only meant to stun subjects rather than injure them, meaning there is no penetration power behind the operator's impact. Because of this, open-handed techniques are often used in a series of combinations to handle a threat.

FORWARD OPEN-HAND STRIKE

Jim Wagner subdues a weaker subject by striking him with the palm of his hand. Using the lead hand, Wagner's left hand travels in a straight line to make contact with the subject's face. Legally, this is a "slap" and not an "arm strike," a distinction, which is more strongly defined in the next photograph.

Jim Wagner has just hit a weaker subject with a forward open-hand strike. Immediately on contact, his impacting hand drops downward to dissipate the force behind the attack. As there is no penetration power behind the impact, the "slap" only stuns the subject rather than injures him.

HORIZONTAL OPEN-HAND STRIKE

This open-handed technique hits from left to right in a straight horizontal line, using the lead hand as demonstrated by Jim Wagner.

As soon as his palm makes contact with the weaker subject, Wagner pulls it back to dissipate the energy and not penetrate his target, thus preventing injury.

VERTICAL OPEN-HAND STRIKE

A weaker subject tries to grab Jim Wagner's legs, which gives him the legal right to use self-defense. However, as the man is crouched over, his fighting capacity is already diminished.

An operator can launch two vertical strikes: either upward or downward. Here, Wagner stuns the hostile subject into submission by bringing his hand up and then coming down on his target's head with a palm strike in a straight vertical line.

As soon as Wagner makes contact with his palm, he correctly pulls back his hand to dissipate energy and not penetrate the target.

OPEN-HAND TECHNIQUE EXTRAS

Instead of "pulling the strike," the operator penetrates the weaker subject with the power of impact. Notice how the operator's force pushes the man's head and body back. Because the subject is physically weaker than the operator, this execution of an open-handed attack is forbidden in the Reality-Based Personal Protection system.

If the operator miscalculates the power of his adversary and discovers that the weaker subject submission strikes are not enough to control the person, he should immediately switch to closed-fist techniques.

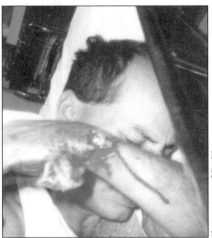

Photo courtesy of Jim Wagner

If the operator can't close his fist because of a broken finger, a bullet wound or other reasons, open-hand strikes that don't dissipate energy are unavoidable. This means that the operator does not "pull a strike"; instead, he hits to penetrate his enemy with power.

This man's wrist was shredded by a K-9. It is so swollen that he is unable to make a fist. In this scenario, the man would have to use an open-hand strike.

ELBOW STRIKES

Elbow strikes are extreme close-range weapons that are especially potent when a hostile subject is within the "red zone," or touching distance of the operator. Of the three distance zones in the Reality-Based Personal Protection system, only friends, family members or lovers should be allowed in the red zone, which is why immediate action must be taken if an adversary penetrates it. Of the two other zones, the orange refers to someone who has to reach out at the operator—be it through a punch, kick or handshake—while the yellow zone refers to someone who has to step in to get the operator or to as far as the operator can see. Obviously, operators must keep all subjects in the yellow zone until restraints are placed on them.

In regards to elbow strikes, like closed-fist and open-hand strikes, there are 10 primary but adaptable techniques.

FORWARD ELBOW STRIKE

REAR ELBOW STRIKE

Forward elbow strikes are not very powerful because they are a straightforward defense. However, they are good to use if an operator must push an attacker backward. To execute, the operator elbows his adversary in the chest by stepping into the strike and pushing it forward in a straight line.

From behind, an attacker grabs and pins the operator's arms to his side. The operator reacts with a swift elbow strike rearward into the attacker's gut, which may break the operator free so he can deal with the conflict head-on.

RIGHT HORIZONTAL ELBOW STRIKE

LEFT HORIZONTAL ELBOW STRIKE

The operator demonstrates a powerful strike on the horizontal plane from a right rear stance. Bringing his elbow up, he strikes the attacker from right to left, rotating his body with the swing to deliver a penetrating blow. Remember that rotation toward the strike's target is essential.

Shown in a left lead stance, the horizontal elbow strike explodes from a cocked position and rotates with the body from left to right.

VERTICAL ELBOW UP STRIKE

VERTICAL ELBOW DOWN STRIKE

Launching the elbow upward, the operator targets either his attacker's chin or lower rib. However, if the operator is lower to the ground, he can also strike upward, targeting his adversary's groin.

With his enemy hunched over, the operator drives the point of his elbow downward and into his target. Remember that a blow is made more powerful by aiming just beyond the point of impact.

DIAGONAL RIGHT and DOWN ELBOW STRIKE

Similar to Thai-kickboxing techniques that use extreme diagonal angles, the strike travels from right to left and up to down. No matter the starting point, the operator brings his elbow up and then strikes it in a downward and slanting direction while rotating to deliver the full force of impact.

DIAGONAL LEFT and DOWN ELBOW STRIKE

Following the opposing diagonal plane from up to down and left to right, the operator brings his left arm up and strikes it to the right in a downward slanting motion. By rotating his body, he creates torque, which helps the operator overcome any turning resistance.

DIAGONAL RIGHT and UP ELBOW STRIKE

Continuing the "X" pattern of the two diagonal planes, this strike goes from down to up and from right to left. The operator stoops and rotates his body while swinging his right elbow to the left in an upward slanting motion to catch the hostile subject in his gut or chest.

DIAGONAL LEFT and UP ELBOW STRIKE

The strike starts from a left lead stance and goes from down to up and from left to right as it hits the attacker. Notice how the operator's body is caught up in the full rotation of the technique.

EMPTY-HAND DEADLY FORCE

A potential tragedy for special-operations and law-enforcement operators is when their firearms malfunction or completely break down. If this happens at a time when the operator needs to use deadly force against an attacker for defense, they may resort to empty-hand deadly force techniques. Here are the most common techniques, which can only be practiced on mannequins for reality-based defense training because of their potency.

TWO-FINGER EYE POKE

The operator executes a deadly force strike. Keeping two fingers together, he shoves them up to the second knuckle into his adversary's eye socket. The attacker's natural reaction will be to look up, which not only exposes him to other fist and kick combinations but also prevents him from harming the operator or stealing his weapon.

FINGER-RAKE EYE GOUGE

The operator rakes his fingers down the attacker's forehead until a finger or two finds the targeted eye socket to execute the empty-hand technique. Notice that deadly force techniques often target the eyes because they are unprotected and require very little power to gouge out.

Photo courtesy of Jim Wagner

In Jim Wagner's Women's Survival course, women are taught to go for the eyes, even if they have boxing gloves, as shown here. Operators must not see eye attacks as something "sissy."

THUMB GOUGE

Once the operator grabs the side of the hostile subject's head, his thumbs automatically enter the eye sockets, even if the head moves.

THROAT GRAB

Wrapping his fingers and thumb around his attacker's esophagus, the operator violently yanks left to right in order to dislodge the organ. To add more force to his grip and keep his adversary in place, the operator catches the man between the legs with a knee and holds him with his free hand.

FORWARD NECK PULL

The operator overlaps his hands behind the attacker's head, but he never interlaces his fingers. To execute this technique, the operator must get his hands set up quickly.

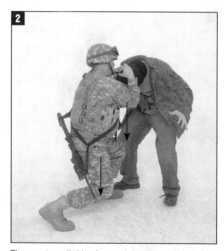

The operator pulls his adversary's head toward his body or literally hangs from the man's head, dropping to his knees and elongating the vertebrae on his own neck to accomplish the move. This is done in one quick motion.

BACKWARD NECK PULL

By somehow ending up behind the attacker, the operator reaches around, overlaps his hands across the enemy's forehead and yanks it backward to break his enemy's neck.

To steady the attacker's head and also control his fall, the operator drives his elbows into the center of the man's back. He then quickly and strongly pulls the head back toward the attacker's own heels.

NECK TWIST

Place one hand on the attacker's chin, but use the other hand to grasp the back of his head. If available, grab his hair or helmet for a more secure grip.

Push the chin with one hand while pulling the head as far as it will go in the opposite direction with the other hand. Enough force must be applied to break the neck instantly.

BLOCKING

More often than not, an operator will have a weapon in his hand at the time of an attack, and even if the weapon malfunctions or has run out of ammunition, that weapon can still be used to block. Because of this, all operators should learn how to use their firearms for defensive blocking. As with other arm strikes in the Reality-Based Personal Protection system, there are 10 practical blocks.

FORWARD BLOCK

With the muzzle of his weapon, the operator performs a sternum strike (See page 72.), which blocks his adversary's potential attack.

REAR RETREAT

Here, the operator gains more reaction time by moving away from an armed attacker. Although not a block in the true sense of the word, moving backward to get away from an attack is a viable defensive-tactical option.

HORIZONTAL INSIDE BLOCK

As the attacker comes in with a knife strike, the operator blocks to the inside by moving his weapon toward the centerline of his body. Remember that a firearm is often carried by a person on their right or left side, which means that it sits on the outside of the body's center.

HORIZONTAL OUTSIDE BLOCK

For this horizontal technique, move away from the body's centerline. Because it is a block, the rifle moves only to push the threat away. Also remember that the rifle will only go as far as the sling allows it.

VERTICAL UP BLOCK

The adversary attacks downward with a knife, but the operator prevents him from making contact with his target by raising a weapon in a rapid upward motion.

VERTICAL DOWN BLOCK

The opposite of up is down on the vertical plane. In this case, the attacker comes up with a knife and the operator meets it with a downward block.

DIAGONAL BLOCK (LEFT and UP)

The diagonal block is not very different from a horizontal block other than perhaps coming up a bit higher and angling the weapon. What truly separates the two techniques is that a horizontal block strikes at the shoulder level, while a diagonal block is easier to angle for a hit to the head.

DIAGONAL BLOCK (RIGHT and UP)

This diagonal block is also considered an outside block because the blocking weapon is moving away from the operator's centerline.

DIAGONAL BLOCK (LEFT and DOWN)

The operator sees a knife coming at him low on a diagonal path and meets the threat by slamming the rifle down and outward.

DIAGONAL BLOCK (RIGHT and DOWN)

The attacker is trying to cut the operator's femoral artery or groin, but the operator pushes the rifle down and away from him at a diagonal angle.

SPECIALTY BLOCKING

While the previous techniques covered the 10 most common angles from which an operator can defend against an attacker, it is still important to understand that some of those techniques can be used for special self-defense situations.

FORWARD SHIELD BLOCK

When an operator has little time to react, he can defend himself against an attack by simply raising his rifle to block the blow.

SIDE SHIELD BLOCK

Although extremely rare, some adversaries do learn traditional-based martial arts and are adept at high kicks. To block, an operator simply reacts with a hard horizontal block.

Although the primary purpose of a rifle is shooting, it is still a machine subject to malfunctions, or it can simply run out of ammunition. For this reason, using it as an impact weapon should be a part of any operator's training program.

Photo courtesy of Jim Wagner

This sign hangs in the 1st Marine Division Scout/Sniper School in Camp Pendleton, where Jim Wagner both learned and taught courses.

Photos courtesy of Jim Wagner

A U.S. soldier strikes his instructor (Jim Wagner) in the sternum and will follow up with a butt strike from his sniper rifle.

FRONT LEG STRIKE ON RESISTORS

Many times when an operator enters a room, an "unknown," or a person who is not displaying weapons at the time of contact, might not comply with lawful orders. That does not mean the unknown is unarmed, rather it's just that they are unknown. Obviously in special operations, every unknown is treated as if they could have a concealed weapon. In situations in which an unknown won't follow orders, the operator must launch a kick into the pelvic area in order to drop his target before the situation necessitates more serious force. It is also important to note that unarmed unknowns may plan to forcibly take the operator's weapon. This is also why a kick is useful because the operator can immobilize his adversary while keeping his weapon pulled to the rear, or at a safe distance.

IDENTIFYING UNKNOWNS

The operator issues clear verbal orders to a hostile subject to get down on the ground. The subject is an "unknown" because he could have a concealed weapon.

The unknown doesn't comply with orders, but he does not posture for a fight, thus making him a "passive resistor." Now, the operator must move in to handle the situation.

As an "active resistor," the unknown openly challenges the operator by threatening him with his empty hands. This means the operator must move in and decide on the appropriate amount of force to control him with. Remember: Appropriate force is based on a real-life fluid combat situation in which less than lethal weapons—like bean bag projectiles, pepper spray and taser guns—may not be available.

COMBAT GLIDE

The operator moves toward the unknown by rolling his feet on the ground heel to toe. The top half of the body stays steady, like a tank turret, while only the legs move like shock absorbers. For civilians, this technique is called the conflict glide only because it softens the term's tone for courtroom situations.

FRONT LEG STRIKE

The operator thrusts the flat of his foot into the pelvic target. This is where a person's center of gravity is, and a kick to that area has the power to drop him. Note that before kicking, the operator draws a "line in the sand" or a launching point for his strike while he approaches the unknown.

This time, the operator is armed with a pistol instead of a long gun while confronting a passive resistor. The operator gives orders to the unknown to get down, but if the unknown does not obey, the operator will kick him.

An active resistor is treated in the same manner. The operator combat-glides toward the unknown and mentally draws the "line in the sand" from where he will launch his front kick.

As the operator moves forward, he thrusts a front kick into the active resistor's pelvic area. Notice that the handgun is kept back and protected from the unknown's reach.

TAKEDOWN

Real-world photo of Officer Jim Wagner with the Costa Mesa Police Department (1998) making an arrest.

Once the unknown is stunned, the operator grabs his shirt, arm or hair and forces him to the ground. While doing this, the operator must also keep his weapon out of reach.

ARREST

Photo courtesy of Jim Wagner

If the operator has backup, he will back off to cover the arresting officer. Remember that the conflict is not over until the adversary is handcuffed and extracted.

FRONT KICK FOR APPROACHES

Although it is important to know how to do an effective front kick from a static position, most special operation's entry-team scenarios are dynamic and involve movement—either by the operator or the enemy approaching the operator. In the following two scenarios, the trainee is equipped with a kicking shield for his protection. The first involves an operator approaching the hostile subject, while the second shows the hostile subject advancing on the operator.

SCENARIO 1

For training with a cleared weapon, the operator approaches the hostile unknown and gives him orders to get down on the ground. Because the unknown is a passive resistor, he does not comply.

As the operator nears, he pulls his long gun back so the unknown will not be able to grab it. The operator is careful to index his weapon to avoid negligent discharge.

Once the operator is in the red zone or striking distance, he launches a front thrust kick into the passive resistor's pelvic area with the flat of his foot. This potent kick will effectively drop most hostile subjects.

The operator uses a front thrust kick to force a door open at a live-fire range.

Photo courtesy of Jim Wagner

SCENARIO 2

The operator enters a room and gives the unknown verbal orders to get down on the ground. The active resistor refuses to obey his lawful order.

Because the hostile subject is an active resistor, he approaches the operator even though he has received verbal orders as well as the international hand signal to stop. Because of this behavior, the operator must quickly decide where to draw "a line in the sand" so that he is prepared to kick.

As the unknown gets within grabbing range of the weapon (the red zone), the operator pulls his long gun out of reach to protect it. The active resistor is about to "cross the line."

The operator launches a thrust kick using the sole of his boot to penetrate the pelvic area in order to stop the aggressing unknown. The weapon stays back during this powerful kick.

Once the unknown is down, the operator makes an arrest. However, if the operator is alone in the room with the unknown, he needs to call out for assistance: "I need two operators for one unknown arrest!"

STOP KICK

If the unknown tries to kick the operator in the pelvic area, the operator jams the incoming kick by bringing his lead foot up and sideways in front of his own centerline.

STOP KNEE

If the attacker has martial arts training, he is more likely to throw kicks by bringing his leg up higher. The operator brings up his lead knee to his centerline to block the kick.

CHAPTER 2

ROOM-ENTRY DEFENSE AND RECOVERY

One of the most dangerous tasks that a special-operations or law-enforcement operator can perform on the job is being part of a stack. A stack is a line of operators ("belly buttons to butts") who are lined up in a team and must go quickly through a door into a room where the enemy could ambush them. I know these high-risk situations very well because I have been the point man in a stack many times.

Obviously, the point man is the most at risk in these situations because he is likely to take hostile fire first. However, there are other risks associated with entering a room. For instance, the enemy might be unarmed on the other side of the door and may try to take the operator's weapon. Or the enemy might be armed with a knife or impact weapon in order to injure the first operator who penetrates the room. The possibility is also high that the enemy is hiding in the hard corners, or "blind spots"—the spaces to the door's immediate left and right, which an operator will not be able to see before entering.

The truth is that room entries are dangerous. It is impossible for the first operator to know exactly where the ambush is coming from without observing beforehand through nano robots, fiber optics, etc; and in most cases, only one operator can enter through the door at a time and only look in one direction. Of course, good team tactics will give the enemy less decision-making time, but the risk of a team member going down can never be completely eliminated. Therefore, I devote this chapter to room entries. Whether on a SWAT team, Hostage Rescue Team or Emergency Reaction Team, or even just as a patrol officer searching for a burglar, these defensive techniques will greatly enhance your personal safety.

DOOR AMBUSH PISTOL GRAB BY UNARMED SUBJECT

Although operators are well armed during a room entry, an adversary lying in wait for an ambush might not be. That's why an operator in an entry team must have highly honed decision-making abilities that rapidly go up and down the use-of-force continuum. (See Appendix 1.) In door ambushes, the attacker lies in wait for the moment the operator penetrates the room in order to steal his weapon.

A two-person entry team enters a room in a stack, but they don't see the unarmed attacker waiting to ambush them. The point man is armed with a secondary weapon (a pistol), while his teammate is armed with a primary weapon (a long rifle).

The point man enters the room and takes the hard left corner when the unarmed attacker tries to wrestle control of the operator's pistol to use against the team. Notice that the second entry-team member has entered behind the point man and immediately scans the opposing hard corner.

The point man anticipated a door ambush, and uses his left hand to push the attacker's hands away from the weapon. To guard his pistol, the point man always keeps it close to his body.

The ambush happened within mere moments of the team's entry, which is why scenario training is so important. No matter their position in a stack, operators must learn how to deal with a lot of door ambushes during training sessions. Meanwhile, the second entry-team member covers his teammate during the struggle because his initial sweep of the hard right corner showed that it was not secure.

The point man pushes the attacker away from his weapon and fires his pistol. Deadly force is acceptable in this situation because the attacker wants the operator's weapon so he can use it against him.

With the door ambush resolved, the entry team quickly scans for other targets before the point man moves in to secure and cover the downed attacker. "If you catch him, you clean him" is the rule, so the shooter's attention is never diverted from the downed, but still potentially dangerous, enemy. The point man will cover his wounded adversary until another operator arrives to arrest the man.

Throughout this situation, the second entry-team member never forgets his responsibility to stay focused and deal with other attackers from the unsecured area. However, if the point man were in serious trouble, the second operator would turn to help him.

If the entry team thinks the situation is not secure after the ambush because they have discovered a bomb on the body or more hostile subjects in the location, they exit from the room quickly.

JIM WAGNER DOOR THRESHOLD ROLL

It is considered "suicide" to clear a room alone, but it happens. For sole operators dealing with simultaneous threats, I've developed a technique by combining a counterterrorist drill, the quick-peek technique, and my own experience to help them because I've also experienced many room entries by myself. This defensive tactic allows lone operators to minimize their exposure time while they look into the left and right hard corners for hidden adversaries.

With no teammates present, the operator enters a room by himself, but he doesn't know that an unarmed attacker is waiting to ambush him on the other side.

Anticipating an ambush, the lone operator scans the interior of the room as much as possible before he moves toward the door. He then steps up to the threshold, but he does not commit himself to entering the room yet.

The operator quickly peeks to the right, although a quick peek to the left is just as valid. The truth is that the operator has a 50-50 chance of finding the attacker on either side of the door.

To peek into the room while on the threshold, the operator quickly rolls his upper body instead of slowly turning his entire body. In real time, it should take less than a second to scan the hard corners.

The operator keeps his index finger straight along the trigger to avoid inadvertent warning shots during this tense situation. Upon properly identifying the target, he immediately shoots a double tap, meaning two shots to the attacker's chest, or a triple tap, meaning two shots to the attacker's chest and one to the head.

Because the situation is so volatile for a lone operator, he correctly extracts himself from the room to find a secure position where he can observe the downed attacker and wait for help to arrive.

ENTRY TRAINING ENVIRONMENTS

Photo courtesy of Jim Wagner

Tire houses are used for live-fire room-entry training.

Photo courtesy of Jim Wagner

Wooden shoot houses look a little more realistic for live fire situations.

Photo courtesy of Jim Wagner

Combat towns, like this U.S. Marine facility, are made of concrete blocks.

Photo courtesy of Jim Wagner

Scenarios in condemned buildings are perfect for FX rounds or air-gun training.

DOOR AMBUSH LONG-GUN GRAB BY UNARMED SUBJECT

Regardless of how well armed a point man is going into a room, there is always the risk of a door ambush. This is why entering with long guns only gives the attacker a larger target to grab. Because a point man may only have a primary weapon like a long gun to use during a room entry, it is vital that operators train for the possibility of this ambush.

In this segment, I explain the muzzle-grab-drop-and-shoot technique, which is also covered in the chapter on "Weapon Retention." However, this chapter emphasizes defensive-team tactics rather than the individual-defensive tactics of the following chapter.

A two-person entry team moves to enter a room, but they are unaware that an unarmed attacker is intent on taking one of their weapons. Here, the point man carries a long gun, or primary weapon, while the second entry-team member carries a pistol, or secondary weapon.

The point man enters and has minimal time to react when the attacker lunges for the gun. Notice that upon entering, the point man went left to take the hard corner while his teammate went right to secure the other hard corner.

During the struggle, the second entry-team member focuses on his area of responsibility and secures the right hard corner as well as the rest of the room. Only when he is done can he pay attention to the commotion on his left.

While the second entry-team member maneuvers to get a clean shot of the attacker, the point man does a muzzle-grab-drop-and-shoot technique. (See page 74.)

The second entry-team member finds a position and fires at the attacker. Notice that he will make sure his partner is not in the way or might unexpectedly stand up by shouting a warning.

Once the hostile subject is down, the shooter secures and covers the body while his teammate conducts a more comprehensive search of the room or arrests the wounded attacker. Another option is that a dedicated snatch team, a group that specifically handles arrests for entry teams, can be brought in instead.

JIM WAGNER ROOM-ENTRY HISTORY

Photo courtesy of Jim Wagner

Jim Wagner first learned room-entry tactics as a police officer. He carried out hundreds of entries.

Photo courtesy of Jim Wagner

As a SWAT officer, Jim Wagner learned more about advanced tactics and working with a team.

Photo courtesy of Jim Wagner

Jim Wagner (left) learned Israeli-style room entries. Here, he is at the famous Wingate Institute.

Photo courtesy of Jim Wagner

Since 1991, Jim Wagner has trained more than 100 special operations teams in room-entry tactics.

VICTIM RESCUE

A tragic reality in special operations is that sometimes a team member goes down, meaning they are injured or even killed. When this happens, the team member becomes a victim. As such, it is necessary for other members of the entry team to evacuate the victim from the hostile area, but that might not be easy if the victim is in the "kill zone," which is the area where a person can still get hit with bullets and fragmentation. To cope in these situations, every member of a tactical team must be well trained in victim-rescue techniques, combat first aid and CPR. Recertification is not only an obligation; it also involves serious attention, which is something I have learned from my own experience in which I've had to administer CPR twice. Also note that although this book focuses on defensive tactics for special operations, a good defensive-tactics program can't ignore post-conflict training, which is why I am including these sections on victim rescue and combat first aid.

An attacker wounds an operator with an AK-47. Injured or dead, the operator's team members must evacuate him from the area.

Abandoned by the attacker, the wounded operator, or victim, is spotted by a friendly operator. Caution is important because the area is still considered a combat zone.

The friendly operator, or rescuer, administers the ABCs of first aid—airway, breathing and circulation—which means he checks the victim's airway, sees whether he is breathing and feels for a pulse. Because the victim is alive, the rescuer decides he needs immediate evacuation.

If there are any hostile activities, the rescuer provides protection first. If this is the case, the rescuing operator puts himself between the threat and the downed victim.

The evacuation process begins when the rescuer grabs the drag handle found on the back of the victim's Load Bearing Vest and pulls the victim out of the area.

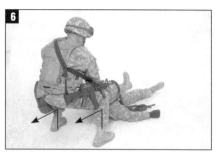

The rescuer initiates the drag with his legs to get the victim moving. He never uses his back, which might cause self-injury.

Once they are in a safe area, the rescuer triages the victim. The friendly operator may have to remove all of the victim's equipment in order to make the victim more comfortable.

With the equipment removed, the rescuer looks for all entrance and exit wounds. Keep in mind that bullets or fragmentation might ricochet around inside the body and exit from an unexpected area.

For any kind of bleeding, the rescuer applies direct pressure followed by a pressure bandage placed over the open wound. A quick-clot agent may also be required.

Once bandaged and treated for shock, the rescuer immediately evacuates the victim to a medical facility. From the moment the friendly operator finds the injury to the moment the victim is delivered to a hospital is considered the "golden hour" of time that determines life or death. That is why the operator wants to move fast.

HAND-GRENADE DEFENSE

One of the realities of modern terrorism and low-intensity conflicts is the use of hand grenades, even by civilian criminals, to carry out crimes and personal crusades. Unfortunately, not all military personnel or civilian law-enforcement agencies are currently learning defensive tactics against these attacks. This reality-based section on hand-grenade defense will be useful in providing life-saving tactics. In order for reactions to be rapid, however, it is important to practice the techniques in real time against an "enemy" who has a simulated grenade in his hand.

Two operators in the imminent conflict stance confront an adversary armed with a hand grenade. Fortunately, the weapon is clearly visible in the hostile subject's hands.

Advancing on the operators, the adversary pulls the hand grenade's safety pin. With the handle or spoon released, the grenade will explode within three to five seconds.

With little time to react, the operators shoot without warning so the attacker doesn't throw the hand grenade at them or others in the area.

After downing the attacker, they yell: "Grenade!" Then, the teammates immediately turn away from the dropped grenade.

The teammates take a big step away from the hand grenade and dive to the ground, which for the purposes of this picture, is closer than it would be in real life. Learning to fall is taught in Jim Wagner's Ground Survival course. (See Appendix 2.)

Pointing the soles of their boots toward the grenade, the operators' feet and legs protect their upper bodies from the explosion and will absorb any shrapnel that does skim across the ground and hit them.

Before the explosion, they close their eyes to keep out dust and debris and cover their ears to prevent ruptured eardrums. The operators also keep their mouths open in order to equalize the air pressure when the bomb explodes.

Immediately after the explosion, the operators recover and secure the wounded or dead attacker because a living one is still capable of launching another attack.

Once in a safe area, the operator performs a self-triage because his close proximity to the explosion may have caused injuries.

SELF-TRIAGE AND SELF-FIRST AID

After a knife fight, gunfight or explosion, many people don't realize that they are injured because they didn't feel the weapon or shrapnel penetrate their body during these adrenalin-filled situations. This perceptual distortion phenomenon is very common in conflict and is why it's important to know that you can be injured even without your knowledge.

When in the field, even in training exercises, find a safe area to perform self-triage and self-first aid in a systematic manner so as not to miss any potential injuries. If with an untrained person, also perform a check on his body for potential injuries that he might have without his knowledge. Remember that injuries are always a possibility in real combat, which is why self-triage and self-first aid are as much a part of defensive tactics as the fighting aspect.

A hand grenade exploded nearby. Do a quick visual search of your body while looking for the obvious: blood, lacerations or missing appendages.

Start from the head and systematically work your way down to the feet while looking for injuries.

As the first part of your systematic search, press lightly on all parts of your head and neck with open hands; it will help you find internal injuries. After you have checked this area, look at your hands for blood.

If you are right-handed, extend your left arm out to the side and check it with the right hand. Start with the armpit, then pat down the rest of the arm while looking at the feeling hand. If you are left-handed, start this procedure on your right arm with your left hand. Check both arms using this step.

Check for torso wounds in the chest and abdomen by pressing firmly on your front side. You may have to remove some equipment and clothing to accurately locate the injury.

With the back of your hands, check the kidney area and the spine. Because it will obviously be difficult to check the upper-back area, have a partner do that for you later.

Check your groin area, especially the arteries extending down your inner thigh. If you are checking an unconscious victim, do not feel embarrassed to check this area of the body.

Pat down your left leg to the knee and then check your hands for blood. If you find no injuries, continue down the rest of the leg. After checking both legs, check your feet. Obviously, you should seek medical help after finishing your self-triage.

SWAT students practice self-triage during a course.

Photo courtesy of Jim Wagner

Once a wound is found, immediate first-aid (training) is required.

Photo courtesy of Jim Wagner

PROTECTING A BABY OR CHILD IN A HAND-GRENADE ATTACK

Once while I was training a military unit, a student asked me how a person would protect a baby or child during a hand-grenade attack. It was a good question that I didn't have an answer for because there were no specific techniques to deal with the scenario, real or not, at the time. So I came up with my own reality-based technique by combining bodyguard, grenade and defensive tactics with advice from medical doctors I had consulted.

While it is uncommon for operators who are rescuing children to be attacked with a hand grenade, today's conflicted world still makes this defense a useful, simple and easy-to-remember technique, especially when practiced from time to time. Using a life-size baby doll, because it is the most realistic way to train, I will take you through my original defensive technique.

As an operator in a conflict situation, Jim Wagner is tasked to rescue a 4-month-old infant.

While conducting the rescue, Wagner sees a hand grenade near his position. For the sake of this demonstration, the grenade is closer to the operator than in real life.

The baby or child must be held in a position that faces the operator. Infants especially must have their head supported to prevent any neck injuries while being handled.

Wagner drops to his knees because a soft landing is imperative in avoiding injuries to the infant. He does not dive. A firm cradling position is also required.

With his back toward the hand grenade, Wagner carefully lands on his forearms using the back of his hands to shield the infant from the impact with the ground.

To protect the infant, Wagner bridges it with his body and does not put any direct body weight on it. He also closes his legs and points the soles of his boots toward the blast area.

Wagner covers the baby doll's ears, and in a real scenario, he would also cover the infant's eyes with his index fingers and put his thumbs in the baby's mouth to keep it open. This leaves the operator at risk for injury, but it does save the baby's life.

Photo courtesy of Jim Wagner

Reality-Based Personal Protection instructor Genny Bloemenhart of Holland learns to protect her child during a Crime Survival course taught by Jim Wagner and Mike Constantinides in Amsterdam.

Photo courtesy of Jim Wagner

"Suspect" Debbie Womack has her child (a doll) rescued during a SWAT scenario.

CHAPTER 3

WEAPON RETENTION

A situation that involves a special-operations operator and an unarmed hostile subject usually ends in favor of the operator because most people will comply with lawful orders when challenged at gunpoint. However, some unarmed adversaries will try to take the operator's weapon and use it against him, which is why weapon-retention training on a regular basis is imperative.

Weapon retention refers to how an operator retains his weapon while someone is trying to take it away from him by force. Operators must maintain the utmost diligence in guarding their weapons, whether primary or secondary, and always assume that an unarmed attacker wants to seize the weapon. However, reality-based retention techniques must be easy to learn and teach, and they should rely on gross-motor skills instead of fine-motor skills. This is because stress in the combat zone makes complicated retention tactics too difficult to remember and perform in a crisis situation.

The key to weapon-retention defensive tactics is that fancy moves will get you killed, which is why traditional martial arts techniques won't work for special-operations or law-enforcement professionals. Anytime an unarmed adversary seizes a firearm, the implied intent is that he is going to use the weapon to seriously injure or kill you. In most cases, deadly force is legal, but it still amazes me that defensive-tactics instructors at police academies or veteran police officers continue to use controlling or impact-force techniques. Here is a common example:

A criminal approaches a law-enforcement officer who is armed with a pistol located in the holster on his gun belt. With both hands, the criminal reaches for the pistol grip of the officer's weapon and tries to rip it out of the holster. The average police officer is usually taught to push the pistol back down into the holster with his weapon hand, knock the criminal's arms away with a downward strike from his free hand and spin out of the attacker's hold at the same time. Officers are also sometimes taught to push or punch the criminal's face while holding onto his weapon and rotating out of his attacker's grip.

From a tactical point of view, pushing the pistol back down into the holster is correct, but the problem with the other techniques is that they will not stop a determined hostile subject. How long does it really take for an attacker to rip a gun out of a police officer's holster? The answer is only a second or two, especially if that person has practiced. The second problem with academy weapon-retention techniques is that the use of force is not proportional. In the example, the criminal uses deadly force to steal the pistol, while the officer merely hits his arms away or strikes him in the face, which can be considered impact force at best. Proportionally, the criminal's force is much higher than the officer's applied force, and that is precisely why so many officers get their own firearms taken away from them during physical altercations and are shot each year.

Of my professional students, many are initially shocked with the simple answer that deadly force is acceptable. "Our administration will never allow it," they often say. Then I remind them that their attacker is using deadly force against them, and suddenly they see that these defensive tactics do fall within the parameters of the law and their various departments' use-of-force policies. After all, doesn't an officer or special agent have the right to defend himself or herself with deadly force, especially if serious injury or death is imminent? When an attacker tries to steal a weapon, danger could not be more so, and for some officers—because of size, gender or handicap—they are no match for an enemy who is willing to murder them to get what they want. In the end, these hardened criminals will easily withstand an officer or operator's few blows to the arms or face because of their stronger motivation to succeed in a conflict situation.

I believe that one reason police academies and military police schools teach watered-down techniques is because of political correctness. It seems as if there is something about eye gouges and throat grabs that administrators don't like, so instead, they use techniques that are more palatable to the public and not as "brutal." Of course, I believe certain techniques should only be used in their appropriate situations, but professionals need to understand that deadly force techniques like eye gouging are legitimate when their life is in immediate danger, especially if a person is trying to kill them with their own gun. Sure, academies and schools often teach their recruits how to double-tap an armed subject with a firearm, but when it comes to defensive tactics, they rarely apply the same rules, even though more officers are involved in hand-to-hand conflicts than shootings. As I've often said to my peers over the years, many law-enforcement agencies just don't seem knowledgeable of the fact that they should spend money on a good realistic defensive-tactics training program.

As a reality-based defensive-tactics instructor, I teach my students gun retention at all costs because they have to do what they need to do in order to survive. Unlike the pistol-in-the-gun-belt example, this section demonstrates how operators who have their weapon on a sling, whether they are an entry-team member with a submachine gun or a scout/sniper with a free-carrying weapon, can appropriately protect them. However, because weapons vary from team to team, mission to mission and individual operator to individual operator, the following techniques are effective for the three main firearm categories: handguns, submachine guns and long guns.

Photo courtesy of Jim Wagner

Jim Wagner teaches civilians how to do a door ambush against a gunman. Such training can prove valuable if an operator loses his or her firearm.

BASIC WEAPONS POSITIONS

To start, I'll begin with the basic weapons positions. Remember that learning to handle and deploy your weapon properly during a mission will help you better retain and recover it after an attack.

LOW READY POSITION

Long View: The operator uses this position when listening for instructions or in situations in which he isn't covering anyone. The gun points at the ground, but the operator always remains attentive.

Close View: In special operations and law enforcement, there is no such thing as accidental discharge; instead, it is negligent discharge. This is why the operator's index finger is placed on the receiver and not the trigger.

HIGH READY POSITION

Use this position to still see the entire body of a hostile subject who is at gunpoint. The weapon's front sight is lined up just below the chin line.

SHOOTING POSITION

An operator uses this position only if he needs to shoot. He uses the weapon's sights by placing them on the center mass of a target.

WEAPON TRANSITION

To transition between primary and secondary weapons, the operator slings the long gun to the rear in order to deploy his pistol.

The secondary, or backup, weapon is a pistol. It is always located in a convenient, easy-to-get-at place. Here, the operator takes it out of his Load Bearing Vest.

LOW READY POSITION

Like the long gun, use this position for a secondary weapon when listening for instructions or in situations in which you are not covering anyone. Even though the gun is pointed to the ground with his finger indexed along the trigger, the operator remains attentive.

HIGH READY POSITION

To see the entire body of an adversary at gunpoint, use this position with a secondary weapon. The front sight is lined up just below the chin line.

EXTENDED TIME POSITION

Hold the pistol in front of your face, but not to where the slide can hit you, when waiting and covering one or more attackers for long periods of time until they are moved, arrested or searched.

SHOOTING POSITION

With a pistol, stand in a modified isosceles stance with your feet shoulder-width apart, knees slightly bent and arms out straight with your elbows locked.

HQ, 1st SF BN, 19th SPECIAL FORCES GROUP (AIRBORNE), 1st SF
Utah Army National Guard
Camp W.G. Williams (Riverton), Utah 84065-4999

23 May 1994

From: Military Intelligence Detachment
To: D.L. Snowden, Chief of Police

Subj: LETTER OF APPRECIATION

1. Chief Snowden, the MI Det enjoyed the participation of
Officer Jim Wagner during our May 1994 drill period. Officer
Wagner was a valuable asset as a visitor to our unit. During
a live fire exercise utilizing 81mm and 60mm mortars, M60
and M16 weapons, he shared his background in special weapons
and tactics to members of the 19th Special Forces soldiers.
His can-do attitude allowed instant repertoire to be established
with our teams and he would be a welcome guest should he
return to train with our troops.

2. During a follow-on airborne exercise, Officer Wagner's
experience in heliborne operations proved helpful in maintaining
current safety operating procedure. You have a valuable man
as I am sure you are aware. Please contact me in the future if
the MI Det of the 1st Battalion, 19th Special Forces can
assist you in any way.

KENNETH E. GENTRY
Sergeant, U.S. Army

Jim Wagner's first contact with the U.S. Army Special Forces was back in 1994. Since then, he has trained with other special-forces units in the United States and Europe.

JERK-AND-RELEASE TECHNIQUE WITH SUBMACHINE OR LONG GUN

Whether during a door ambush or when the restraints go on, some enemies will seize any opportunity to take the operator's submachine or long gun. Obviously, successful disarmament could mean injury or death to the operator or others, which is why learning to react quickly is what this technique is about.

A hostile subject tries to grab Jim Wagner's long gun, which is a possibility in any of the following circumstances: a door ambush, a meeting with a "friendly" who turns hostile, etc.

Wagner has little time to react and shoot before his adversary grabs his weapon. This brings them into an uncomfortably close proximity because an operator's body is usually attached to the weapon by a sling.

Wagner can use a number of standard techniques to free his weapon—like twisting the rifle, pulling it back or shoving it forward to push his attacker off-balance—but whether he should implement them depends on the situation.

In this case, the operator is unable to free his weapon. The hostile subject has control of the weapon, but because of the sling, he still does not possess it.

Seeing that his attacker has a good grip, Wagner suddenly thrusts his weapon up to around head level. This unexpected and violent upward movement catches his adversary by surprise.

Without loosing momentum, Wagner jerks the weapon toward the ground, bending his knees to get low. He does the entire upward and downward movement in one fluid motion.

The attacker most likely lets go of the weapon because of the violent up-and-down jerk. If he does not, he still will receive a painful jolt to the arms, which will also affect his shoulders.

After the jerk-and-release technique, Wagner must do a follow-up technique to stun the hostile subject, who has merely released the weapon and is capable of another attack.

Wagner strikes with a butt stroke to the attacker's head, which is a smooth follow-up to the jerk-and-release technique. Remember, any time a hostile subject grabs hold of an operator's weapon, the operator may return deadly force with deadly force.

Once the attacker goes down, Wagner backs away while giving orders to the downed subject at gunpoint. Wagner can now call a second operator or a snatch team to make the arrest.

STERNUM STRIKE

If a hostile subject attempts to grab hold of an operator's weapon, a muzzle thrust into the sternum bone is a good stopping-power technique. Obviously, the operator's trigger finger must be indexed alongside the weapon to avoid negligent discharge through a sympathetic-response reflex, like a fist clench under pressure.

Because the attacker attempts to grab the weapon, the operator construes it as a use of deadly force. Remember, attempting to and actually grabbing hold of a weapon are two different things. The former involves an attacker who tries to touch the operator's weapon and fails, which is a situation in which deadly force is not allowed. The latter involves an attacker who succeeds in laying hands on the weapon, which means deadly force is an absolute necessity. In this scenario, a sternum strike does not inflict permanent damage and is not deadly force.

The operator pulls the weapon away before his adversary has the chance to make a better grab for the long gun. But to execute it correctly, the operator's action must be fast and well practiced.

He thrusts the tip of his muzzle into the attacker's sternum bone. Anywhere the muzzle hits, even if it misses the sternum and hits a rib or part of the chest, will be painful and should stop the hostile subject.

If the sternum strike fails because of a thick jacket or because only a large muscle was hit, the operator prepares to use other strikes to stop the attacker.

The butt stroke is an excellent follow-up strike. However, some police agencies and military units have eliminated this technique because the muzzle points at team members who may be behind the operator and there is a chance for negligent discharge.

Once the enemy is no longer resisting, the operator steps back and prepares for the arrest. At a safe distance, the operator gives commands for him to get down.

The operator calls for assistance and covers the prisoner. A second operator comes to his aid and makes the arrest. However, because the arresting officer does a weapon transition, he will have no weapon for safety. That is why the original operator must cover his teammate carefully.

Although there are many ways to handcuff a prisoner, the arresting operator performs a standard police-style arrest, which means the prisoner is made to look in the opposite direction. This prevents the prisoner from seeing the operator's intentions and planning his escape.

The arresting operator orders the prisoner to put his hands on the small of his back. He then pulls the prisoner's arm up by the wrist while resting his knee lightly on the prisoner's neck. The covering operator, meanwhile, remains attentive to other potential dangers.

The prisoner requires medical attention even if no injuries are visible. He may have internal injuries.

MUZZLE-GRAB-DROP-AND-SHOOT TECHNIQUE

Unlike the jerk-and-release technique, the operator loses control of his weapon when an adversary grabs the muzzle. By grabbing the pivot point, the hostile subject can easily control and turn the weapon from himself and keep it off his centerline unless the operator reacts with this technique. Note that it's essential to practice all the elements of the muzzle-grab-drop-and-shoot technique together until they blend into one.

As an operator turns to take a hard corner, which may happen while he searches a closet or small room, a hostile subject prepares to ambush him. This scenario is also possible when a prisoner in a jail cell jumps up and surprises the operator with an attack.

Grabbing hold of the muzzle, the attacker pushes it away from himself so that the operator's aim is unstable, which makes it unsafe to shoot anything. This means that the operator no longer has control of his weapon.

As much as the operator tries to wrestle his weapon back, the attacker maintains control of it. This is a deadly situation for the operator, and he must get out of this struggle at all costs.

If the operator sees that he can't wrestle back his weapon, he immediately drops to one knee. At this moment, the hostile subject still controls the muzzle, but his ability to maneuver it is now limited.

The operator angles the weapon so that the muzzle is pointing directly at his adversary's midsection. He quickly looks down to find the trigger if he cannot find it by feel alone.

Pulling the trigger, he fires into the attacker. Even if the bullets do not hit the target, the shock alone could make the operator's adversary let go of the muzzle. Note: Operators must also remain aware of where, what or who their stray bullets could impact. This is called "backdrop awareness."

After the shots, the operator gets back to his feet instantly and covers the wounded or dead attacker.

As another option, the operator rotates the butt of his weapon toward his adversary's head, which is possible because of leverage.

Justified in using deadly force to retain his weapon, the operator drives the butt of the gun into the attacker's head as hard as possible.

The operator must properly cover the downed hostile subject because he may be armed with a bomb belt, which is a common scenario in this day and age.

MONKEY RELEASE OF PERSONAL WEAPON

In Asia, there is a simple way to catch a monkey by manipulating its natural instincts. A hunter drills a hole the size of the animal's open hand into an empty coconut, puts nuts inside the hollow fruit and secures the coconut to a tree with a rope. When a monkey goes by, it will put its hand into the hole to grab the nuts. However, with its hand clenched around the nuts, the monkey's fist is too large to fit back through the hole, and the monkey is too stubborn to release the food to free itself. Eventually, the hunter will return to put the monkey in a burlap sack and cook it for his dinner that night.

The lesson of this story is: If you can't wrestle your weapon free from the grasp of a hostile subject, don't be like the monkey. Let go of the weapon. Jam your hand up into the attacker's face and gouge out his eyes. Remember, a person who is trying to steal your weapon justifies the use of deadly force.

An attacker surprises an operator to steal his weapon, which is a circumstance that happens under a variety of situations, like an ambush, attempted arrest, etc. Because of the surprise attack, the operator has very little time to pull his weapon away from his enemy's grasp.

The hostile subject can't pull the long gun completely away from the operator because it is on a sling. However, he can still handle and aim the weapon at other operators that may be in the same area as the struggle.

Twisting, pulling and shoving the gun, the operator realizes that he is not going to get his weapon back. But unlike the monkey that won't let go, the operator will let go of his weapon to save himself.

Immediately releasing his weapon, the operator attacks his adversary's eyes with a thumb-eye-gouge technique. Even a criminal in a drug-induced state will let go of anything once his eyes are injured.

The attacker releases the long gun to protect his eyes, which gives the operator a moment to rearm himself. Fortunately in this situation, the sling of the weapon works in the operator's favor by keeping it readily accessible.

To cover the wounded subject and protect the recovered firearm, the operator pulls his weapon back a bit or steps backward.

As the attacker is severely wounded with eye injuries, he voluntarily lowers his body to the ground, but the operator must be aware of any tricks.

If alone, the operator moves up to his adversary and lays his hands on him, but if he is with others, the operator needs to cover his wounded prisoner while a snatch team or teammate carries out the arrest.

If working alone, the operator pulls the attacker downward so he hits the ground chest first. Almost always, a dangerous prisoner is placed on the ground in a police or military operation because it immobilizes him.

Although handcuffs are good restraint tools, all operators should carry 20 or more nylon restraint devices in a cargo pocket just in case they need to arrest a large number of people.

MONKEY RELEASE OF ENEMY WEAPON

Releasing a weapon not only helps an operator retain his firearm but also helps him take control of his adversary's weapon. If you find yourself in a situation in which your own weapon has malfunctioned, use the monkey-release technique to keep from being shot. Here's how it works:

In a struggle to gain control of your adversary's weapon, you must realize when it is time to fight and when it is time to let go. In this case, it is time to let go.

Put your chest up against the hostile subject to deny him any maneuvering room and then release your grip on his weapon. This sets you up for your next goal, which is to immediately go for the eyes.

Do a thumb-eye-gouge technique, but don't do it lightly. Remember that the point of this deadly-force technique is to drive your thumbs deep into your enemy's eye sockets because failure can mean getting shot by him instead.

Execute an arrest after the attacker is down and still alive. If he is alive, the operator will probably have to treat him for shock.

Photo courtesy of Jim Wagner

Confined spaces, such as in this bus, are an opportunity for an attacker to grab an operator's weapon.

Photo courtesy of Jim Wagner

Even maritime environmentalists do not allow operator's the luxury of distance. Instead, they must put weapons close to the hostile subjects.

Photo courtesy of Jim Wagner

Jim Wagner's students of the Helsinki Police learn how to search hostile subjects so a weapon can not be grabbed easily.

Photo courtesy of Jim Wagner

Jim Wagner (rear) observes his GSG9 operators during a training program as "terrorists" try to seize the MP5 submachine guns from the operators.

SINGLE-WEAPON STRUGGLE

Struggling over a single weapon to survive is not a far-fetched idea, and regardless of how he ends up in this position, every operator should include a fight over a single weapon as a necessary part of his training. I routinely have my special-operations students fight over a rubber or plastic firearm, but any training tool (e.g., toy baseball bats, toy hammers or screwdrivers) that is safe is fine. In fact, when I was going through the Federal Law Enforcement Training Center back in 2002, the defensive-tactics instructors had us fight over a single, rigid plastic knife.

In the following sequence, I will demonstrate how to go about this vital exercise, which can be practiced from any position.

In this training exercise, Peter Falk holds the training weapon—a rubber handgun with the trigger guard cut for safety—anyway he wants.

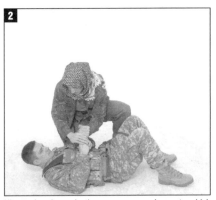

His attacker also grabs the weapon anyway he wants, which makes this training situation more reality-based. It also forces Falk into a position of disadvantage that will test his decision-making skills.

Falk and his adversary fight over the rubber handgun when the training instructor (not shown) yells, "Go!" Falk's goal for this exercise is to shoot his attacker.

The goal of the operator is to keep the enemy between his legs, otherwise known as the "guard position" in wrestling, which helps keep his adversary in front of him.

Once his knee is in place, the operator starts digging his heels into the hostile subject. He then pushes off the subject with his knee only to knock his enemy completely off-balance with his heel or foot.

Once the hostile subject is stunned or injured by the kicks or digs, the operator takes advantage of the situation and rips away the disputed firearm. Remember that in the end, there is no "magic" grab or technique.

Once the weapon is freed, the operator shoots the enemy from his position while lying flat on his back. If there is a malfunction, the operator might have to clear the weapon first before firing at his adversary.

The operator continues to shoot or cover his downed attacker while uprighting himself. Notice that just because the hostile subject is wounded, it doesn't mean he is no longer a threat. He still could be dangerous.

The operator must immediately get to his feet by using a heavy-load-recovery technique. To do the move, sit up, get up on one knee, place your weight over that knee and stand up.

Never turn your back on an enemy when engaged in a ground conflict because the position is vulnerable and exposes your back!

HAND-HELD CHEMICAL-DEVICE ATTACK

In some situations, the operator may encounter a subject who is armed with a portable chemical-admitting device, a term that can include cans of pepper spray, a cup of acid, squeeze bottles with a cleaning agent, or even a cup of urine and feces such as may be thrown in a prisoner-transport situation; this is known as being "gassed." There are two reasons a single adversary might use a chemical against an approaching operator: 1) to make escape possible and 2) to create an opportunity to take the operator's weapon and use it against him or her. When going through counterterrorism school in Artesia, NM, I came up with a technique to defend against these chemical attacks. Since then, I have trained thousands of police and military operators in the same technique.

A man hides a can of pepper spray behind his back and refuses to obey lawful orders. Because the operator doesn't see the chemical weapon, the man is considered an unknown.

By deploying his weapon, the unknown becomes a visible adversary. Because the operator can't identify his attacker's weapon and the situation necessitates that he assume that the weapon contains a deadly chemical, he moves in to employ deadly force.

Before the operator employs deadly force, his attacker sprays his face with pepper spray. Fortunately, the operator manages to block most of the incoming chemical by instinctively raising his arm.

To get away from the cloud of airborne particles and gain more reaction time before the hostile subject moves in to do more harm, the operator immediately moves backward.

During his rapid retreat, the operator places his left biceps over his left eye, which automatically closes both eyes. He also holds his breath so as not to breathe in the toxic chemicals.

The forearms receive the main blast of the chemical agent, while the biceps naturally remain uncontaminated. The operator knows this and wipes his left eye and face one time with his upper arm. Next, he wipes the right eye and face with his right biceps. Note that he can only wipe each side once with each arm because a second time may recontaminate his face.

The attacker pursues the operator during his retreat. The operator must take immediate defensive action regardless of any chemical residue still on his skin.

The operator shoots the incoming attacker because he is in danger of being incapacitated with the chemical agent. Deadly force is authorized, which means the operator shoots to stop him.

Once the attacker is no longer a threat, the operator uses his personal water source to begin the decontamination process. He opens his water tube to rinse his face and any contaminated equipment. If the chemical is dangerous—like sulfuric acid, kitchen cleansers or corosives—he must seek immediate medical attention.

A Helsinki police officer practices Jim Wagner's technique against an inert agent.

Photo courtesy of Jim Wagner

SNIPER JERK AND RELEASE OF A LONG GUN

While training to be a sniper with SWAT, I found few if any techniques that were available to help snipers deal with a hostile subject while deploying their final firing position or observation post. This means that while those specialized operators traveled to the position from which they planned to shoot or observe their target, they had learned no defensive tactics to deal with an unexpected hostile situation. I decided to teach my scout/sniper students defensive tactics when I became a sniper instructor a few years later. Now should they ever run into hostilities, they have unique techniques for their particular missions and equipment to help them deal with attackers.

This particular technique specifically is used when an unknown tries to grab a sniper's specialized rifle: a Remington 700, as shown in the photos.

An unknown subject approaches the sniper while he is trying to get to his final firing position In an urban environment, scout/snipers are often separated from their team.

The unknown is obviously an active resistor because he rapidly advances on the sniper. Attempting to stop him, the sniper issues lawful orders, but it does not work.

Before the sniper can raise his rifle to hit his adversary with it, the active resistor lunges for the sniper's weapon, instantly instigating a deadly-force situation.

Just as the hostile subject grabs the rifle, the sniper quickly throws the gun upward, which is a violent move few aggressors are prepared for. The sniper also wants to throw the weapon up as high as he can to prepare for the next move, which will make his attacker wish he had never grabbed the rifle.

The sniper snaps the rifle as low as he can. This forces the subject to let go of the weapon, or he ends up jarring his fingers, wrists and elbows. Just as fast as the rifle was flung upward, it's equally important for the sniper to pull down even more violently because the sudden change in direction creates a whiplash effect that pops the attacker's shoulders.

With the rifle free from the attacker's grip, the sniper immediately follows up with a butt stroke to his attacker's head. Remember, the use of deadly force is justified.

The sniper comes back across his adversary with a down-stroke strike. In the Reality-Based Personal Protection system, this is a right-handed diagonal-down-backhand strike, although a left-handed strike is just as valid.

After the attacker has stopped, the sniper moves back and takes the subject down at gunpoint. Because sniper rifles are more delicate than regular operator's weapons, remember not to switch to a secondary weapon unless your primary weapon is safely on a sling.

Photo courtesy of Jim Wagner

Jim Wagner (left) and his partner moving to their final firing position during a training exercise at the Marine Corps Base at Camp Pendleton.

SNIPER'S SECONDARY (BACKUP) WEAPON

Although long guns are a sniper's primary weapon, they are not the best self-defense weapon. This is because they are not designed for close-range situations that a sniper might face if he is ambushed while stalking to his final firing position or observation post. It is imperative that every scout/sniper carry a secondary weapon—usually a pistol with an extra magazine—just in case he encounters a hostile subject and his primary weapon is attached to him with a sling. However, the question often asked is, Where should you place the secondary weapon?

In many missions, a sniper has to crawl on his belly to get into position for shooting or observing, which means a gun belt or a leg holster is impractical because it will be dragged through the dirt and mud. In the photos for this segment, I show my own ghillie suit, or special sniper camouflage, which I made while going through the U.S. Marines' advanced scout/sniper course at Camp Pendleton. To accommodate my duty pistol, I sewed in a shoulder holster. This was the best place for my secondary weapon, especially when I was on my plates (the canvas used to keep the suit from ripping or wearing out) in a prone position.

This sniper wears the top half of a ghillie suit while armed with a Remington 700 and a pistol that is sewn into his jacket.

A good ghillie suit is handmade by the operator so it specifically suits the individual's needs and environment; commercial suits are too generic. In this photograph, the operator chose to sew a pistol holster in his jacket.

NO WARNING   NO REMORSE
SCOUT SNIPER SCHOOL

Photo courtesy of Jim Wagner

This painted sign is on a wall at the U.S. Marine Scout/Sniper School.

An armed hostile subject aggresses the sniper, who is moving to his assigned location. The sniper gives a warning, if policy allows, but to no avail. The sniper must use deadly force to stop him.

The sniper has his weapon attached to a sling, so he transitions his weapon behind him and goes for his secondary weapon. The weapon is a pistol under his left armpit.

Because the sniper has practiced for this possibility with a lot of scenario training, he quickly deploys his weapon. Practicing once in a while is never good enough.

The sniper shoots his adversary at close range. This is why he does a point-shooting technique while keeping his weapon canted and close to his body. By tilting and then firing the pistol, the sniper makes sure that the slide operates properly while in near to his body and doesn't get snagged in his ghillie suit. He also keeps his secondary hand up to defend himself.

At such a close range and as long as the pistol is pointed toward the hostile subject's centerline, it is next to impossible to miss. In training, air guns can be used to develop reality-based accuracy and confidence.

The sniper secures the subject until help can arrive. If the sniper is working in a two-person team, his partner can approach the downed subject while the sniper covers him.

CHAPTER 4

HELMET DEFENSE

M̲ost high-risk special-operations operators wear helmets, and those helmets are designed for a variety of situations that include withstanding small-arms fire or protecting the head against a fall or moderate impact. However, one of the drawbacks is that an unarmed attacker can easily grab hold of the operator's helmet, which is strapped to his head, and use it to injure or even kill him with a sharp pull or tug to break his neck. Despite this, no one really taught defenses against this attack before 1992 when I began addressing the situation. In fact, by the time I had perfected my helmet-defense techniques, I was invited by the German government to train their top counterterrorism team, called the *Grenzschutzgruppe Neun* or GSG9, in 1999. These well-trained operators loved the relevance of my helmet-defensive tactics because of their own oversize and easy-to-grab helmets, which were known as "koala ears." Since then, units all over the world continue to adopt these techniques in their own training.

FRONT HELMET-GRAB DEFENSE

If somebody grabs an operator's helmet from the front and jerks it down, or twists it violently from side to side, they could easily break the operator's neck. It was because of the danger of this attack that I developed a technique in 1992 to help operators survive it.

Jim Wagner gives lawful orders to an unknown. Because the situation seems like a low-risk event, Wagner does not stand in the alert conflict stance. However, he also doesn't realize that the unknown is about to become hostile.

The unknown is now the attacker and jumps up reaching for Wagner's helmet. An attack like this can happen in a moment. For an unarmed attacker, the helmet is an attractive and easy-to-grab lure.

The attacker manages to grab the front of the helmet and will pull or twist it to break Wagner's neck unless Wagner reacts immediately. Note: If an operator does not practice the following defensive steps on a regular basis, he will probably not have enough reaction time when such an attack occurs.

Because Wagner has no time to strike or go for a weapon, he immediately brings up his hands and grabs the most visible targets: the attacker's wrists or forearms.

There is no "magic" or proper way to grip the attacker's wrists. Instead, Wagner just grabs what is immediately available, holds on tightly and tucks his chin inward for more neck muscle control.

The operator then violently pulls his adversary's arms down to strip the grip from his helmet. He also turtles his neck to immobilize his head and prevent any strain on the muscles or spine.

Once the hostile subject's hands are stripped away, Wagner pushes him away because a person who grabs a helmet once is more than likely to grab it a second time.

An enemy who tries to control or injure an operator through his helmet is a dangerous person, and as such, Wagner immediately takes him down at gunpoint once he has pushed him back.

If the operator cannot strip the attacker's hands free from his helmet, a knee strike to the subject's pelvic area is imperative.

Two of Jim Wagner's GSG9 students practice helmet defense.

Photo courtesy of Jim Wagner

REAR HELMET-GRAB DEFENSE

Nobody is 100 percent safe from a hostile subject who attacks from behind, especially if it includes a helmet grab that can result in a fatal neck break. This rear defensive technique will help you from losing your head—literally.

An attacker readies a rear ambush for an operator who doesn't realize that he is in danger. This is perhaps because his adversary was missed in an earlier search or approaches him from another location.

Rushing up to the operator, the attacker grabs his helmet from behind. Because the helmet is fastened to the operator's head, he is left immobile during the attack.

The operator grabs his own helmet to protect himself from a severe neck injury, which will happen if the attacker manages to pull it down or twist it.

While under attack, the operator is not concerned with where his adversary's hands are on the helmet. Instead, his goal is to hold his helmet firmly onto his head and prevent it from being used to break his neck.

Firmly holding onto his helmet, the operator rotates 180 degrees because there is simply no time for strikes in this dynamic situation. To help him turn, the operator will hit the attacker with his elbows.

As the operator spins, the hands of the attacker are stripped off his helmet because his turn is violent and quick. Note that the operator tightens the muscles in his shoulders and neck into one unit while he spins.

The operator shoves his attacker away, but obviously, this is the type of person who will try to attack again or even try to go for the operator's weapon.

The operator can follow up with a counterattack—in this case, he uses arm strikes—if the hostile subject is too close. If possible, the operator should seek to back away from the scene.

Remember that the attacker used deadly force by grabbing onto the operator's helmet. Therefore, the operator, once free from his grip, takes the enemy down at gunpoint.

The operator commands his attacker to get down into a prone position and calls for an arrest officer or a snatch team. Despite his aggressive attack, the man is still an "unknown" because he could have concealed weapons.

FRONT HELMET HEAD BUTT

With all the equipment an operator wears, he sometimes forgets that his helmet is not only a solid piece of armor but also a formidable weapon. So note that a head butt with a helmet on, if executed correctly, to an unprotected head can knock out an adversary. I address this rarely used defensive tactic with the following technique.

This technique works on any hostile subject who attacks the operator, either with empty hands or weapons. Here, a masked unknown attacks the operator, Peter Falk. For whatever reason, Falk is not in the alert conflict stance and does not have his weapon in the ready position.

The unknown strikes Falk with a closed fist, but it is blocked.

Because his attacker is too close and the initial ambush was overwhelming, Falk can't deploy his weapon. Falk will wait for a "pause in conflict," or a moment when his adversary will pause to evaluate any damage he caused or damage inflicted by Falk on him.

When the "pause" arrives, Falk grabs the hostile subject's head or shoulders. To create one large impact unit, Falk pulls his upper body—neck, shoulders and spine—back in unison to slam them into the attacker's face.

Using his body weight, Falk strikes his adversary with his helmet. Because he is wearing the helmet, Falk doesn't have to worry about injuring his own head while he cracks open his attacker's skull. Note that in less lethal conflicts, care must be taken to avoid splitting an adversary's skull because they don't warrant deadly force.

Multiple helmet strikes can be done without injury to the operator. Here, Falk pulls back his head for greater momentum.

Once the attacker goes down, Falk arrests his adversary by taking him to the ground. During the arrest, Falk holds his prisoner in place by putting pressure on his back with a knee.

Once the downed attacker is in a prone position, Falk arrests him by telling him to place his hands, one at a time, on the small of his back. Once his hands are in position, Falk pulls them in and handcuffs them.

Photo courtesy of Jim Wagner

Jim Wagner's original techniques on helmet defense have appeared in tactical magazines worldwide.

FRONT HELMET BLOCK

The operator's helmet is good not only for striking but also for blocking incoming strikes. Unfortunately, this technique is terribly overlooked by most defensive-tactics instructors. Combat helmets, riot helmets or even a traffic cop's helmet are a hard shell that can injure a hostile subject's hand, especially if he strikes at it. Operators must get used to this advantage and diligently practice blocking techniques.

An attacker launches an unarmed assault against an operator. However, because of extensive helmet-defense training, the operator sees an opportunity to avoid the attack and self-injury.

Before the strike hits the operator's face, he brings his chin down, causing the attacker to make contact with his hard helmet instead.

Jim Wagner's SWAT students are required to fight in full gear—including helmets. Students soon learn to use them to their advantage.

Photo courtesy of Jim Wagner

Photo courtesy of Jim Wagner

Jim Wagner (right) supervises two special-operations operators. Notice that the operator in black has his helmet stuck, preventing him from escaping. Contact scenarios teach you unforgettable lessons.

CHAPTER 5

KNIFE DEFENSE

In the early 1990s, I offered a defensive knife-training course to my SWAT teammates only to have my sincere offer met with amusement. My colleagues believed that as long as they had their guns, no one could hurt them. Basically, they thought a gun was always superior to a knife and an officer did not need to worry about knife attacks as long as he had his pistol, or in the case of my SWAT team, MP5 submachine guns. In fact, my offer was turned down again even after my agency's team had an officer stabbed through the arm with a screwdriver by a burglary suspect because he didn't have enough time to draw his weapon.

The sad truth is that many police officers and soldiers think they are impervious to knife attacks just because they're carrying "the big guns." Yet, I've instructed, trained with and been involved with countless special-operations personnel who have proved that operators can be severely injured or killed by a surprise knife attack. A case in point is when Sgt. Dan Powers, a 12-year Army veteran, was investigating a site with his squad in East Baghdad in 2007. Even though he was heavily armed, an Iraqi insurgent came up through a crowd and buried a knife eight inches deep into Powers' skull. At the time, Powers thought that he had merely been punched, so he slammed his attacker to the ground. It is fortunate that Powers survived the encounter because surgeons were able to remove the weapon from his brain.

Granted, such an attack usually won't happen if all firearms are trained on a single adversary, but operators do tend to get into trouble in ambushes, if a weapon malfunctions or during arrest-and-control techniques. (See Chapter 7.) Despite initial skepticism, the one class that has gotten my foot in the door with more agencies and units than any other has been my Knife Survival course. With it, I've trained elite forces like the U.S. Marshals Service Special Operations Group, the GSG9, the Israeli Special Forces, the German Special Forces and many more because, as the years pass, more and more units are seeing the need for knife-survival tactics in special-operations training.

This is the official logo of Jim Wagner's Knife Survival course, a popular knife program that is taught around the world.

UFC LEGEND MATT HUGHES: *Exclusive Interview!*

BLACK BELT.

WORLD'S LEADING MAGAZINE OF MARTIAL ARTS

SURVIVAL GUIDE
JIM WAGNER ANSWERS YOUR QUESTIONS ABOUT REALITY FIGHTING

DOGFIGHT!
KARATE VS. CANINES

42 ESSENTIAL LESSONS
FROM THE TOP TEACHERS OF THE MARTIAL ARTS

+ BLADES VS. BARE HANDS
SPORT SAMBO SUBMISSIONS
JEET KUNE DO WITH GARY DILL

01043 FEBRUARY 2008
www.blackbeltmag.com
$4.99US $6.99CAN

7 25274 01043 1

Cover photo by Rick Hustead

The cover of the February 2008 issue of *Black Belt* features Jim Wagner, who appears in his Army combat uniform. He received permission to appear in uniform from the California State Military Reserve, 40th Infantry Division Support Brigade.

WINDSHIELD-WIPER SUBMACHINE GUN DEFENSE

Nothing is worse than pulling the trigger of a powerful weapon that fails to fire—except if it happens while an attacker hacks away at you with a knife. Every operator must train for this possibility, and for more than a decade, I've taught special-operations teams around the world how to use this original technique.

An attacker ambushes an operator with a knife. Unfortunately, the operator's weapon fails to fire and he has no time to deal with the malfunction.

If the operator takes time to check or clear his weapon, the attacker will be on him in a split second, which will prove fatal. There is also no time to transition to a secondary weapon.

Rather than deal with a malfunctioning weapon, the operator reacts with an immediate rifle block. As the rifle is hard, metallic and plastic, there is a good chance that the operator may break his attacker's knife arm.

Because the weapon is on a sling, the operator waves it back and forth like a windshield wiper while making a tactical retreat to gain reaction time.

As the operator waves his primary weapon back and forth and retreats, he quickly goes for his secondary weapon, which in this photo is located on the Load Bearing Vest.

To have this technique work at the "moment of truth," the operator must practice pulling his secondary weapon out over and over again in realistic training scenarios.

The operator then fires rounds into the oncoming attacker, but depending on the situation, he might want to keep a hold of the primary weapon as a moving shield while firing. This means that as he takes the hostile subject down at gunpoint, he continues to wave his long gun as a defense.

Notice the angle of the pistol. The pistol is canted (off to an angle), which is necessary to prevent the slide from hitting the vest and causing a failure-to-feed malfunction.

Once the attacker is downed, the operator will move back to wait for help or cover the prisoner while an arrest officer moves in to secure him. If it was not made clear before, please note that anyone an operator suspects of being armed with a hand-held weapon other than a projectile must be at least 21 feet (seven meters) away for adequate reaction distance. Remember, it only takes two seconds for an attacker to close that distance, which is why this specific measurement is necessary. Obviously, in these pictures, the distance is not shown to scale.

Once the operator is in a safe location, he will clear his weapon and make it mission ready. If there is no time to do so, the operator will use his secondary weapon for the remainder of the mission.

SENTRY REMOVAL

Special-forces units around the world are taught how to sneak up behind an enemy and cut his throat or send a blade through his kidney. Unfortunately, renegade groups like al-Qaida and others study and practice this deadly skill, as well. Although disturbing, this technique will demonstrate how to remove a sentry from his post.

While standing post or having a cigarette break, an operator doesn't notice an armed attacker sneak up behind him who is ready to kill.

Undetected, the silent attacker goes right up to the operator and pulls his helmet back in a violent and snapping manner.

He quickly follows his assault with a blade thrust into the operator's jugular, which instantly incapacitates the victim. In training, like here, attackers use rubber-training knives.

The attacker carefully holds the body and lays it down on the ground gently to muffle any sounds so as not to draw any attention.

Once the body is quietly on the ground, the attacker finishes the job by slitting the operator's throat, which obviously prevents him from calling for help.

The operator is not the main objective of the mission, but merely someone who needs to be eliminated for the operation to continue. The hostile subject looks around to make sure his attack went undetected.

The attacker might end up hiding the body around the corner somewhere so it will not be discovered, or he could simply move on and continue his mission.

The attacker is now free to move on and spread destruction, which is why an operator should never be by himself in a hostile environment. In order to avoid this tragic situation, move on to read about the next technique.

Photo courtesy of Jim Wagner

Photo courtesy of Jim Wagner

Morné Swanepoel, the director of the Reality-Based Personal Protection program in South Africa, practices sentry removal.

A German student tries a variation of the technique by covering the mouth and nose of his victim and pressing hard.

SENTRY REMOVAL DEFENSE

Military books around the world show how one can remove a sentry, but they don't show sentries how to defend themselves against the technique. Having been an operator, I train my students in sentry removal and in sentry defense. The following technique demonstrates the same tactic I teach to elite police and military units.

A silent attacker sneaks up on a sentry. Note: A good sentry stays alert at all times because he knows an attack can and will happen regardless of his post.

Because the sentry is alert, he periodically follows the golden tactical rule: "Stop. Look. Listen." He hears a slight noise coming up behind him.

The moment the sentry sees anything in his peripheral vision or feels anything, he immediately turns in the direction of the threat, bringing up both hands in defense.

Immediately, the sentry pushes away the threat, which in this case is an attacker with a combat knife. In training exercises, this movement should be repeated many times for muscle memory.

Next, the sentry backs away from the knife because in a knife fight, distance is your friend. This will also give the operator more reaction time to get to his own weapon.

With some distance between himself and his attacker, the sentry readies his weapon while moving back. If the arm that carries his primary weapon is wounded by the knife, the sentry might have to use a secondary weapon for protection.

The sentry, who has clearly identified the target, fires at his attacker while moving back 21 feet (seven meters) to gain a minimum-reaction distance.

Once it is safe to move up on the downed enemy, or as the situation dictates, the operator will check and clear the body for explosives and other weapons.

Jim Wagner not only teaches defense against knives but also designs them. The Jim Wagner Reality-Based Blade made by Boker is one of the top selling tactical folders on the market.

Photo courtesy of Jim Wagner

THE JIM WAGNER KNIFE-DISARM RULE

Before 1997, police academies, militaries and martial arts schools tended to teach knife disarms, which consisted of dozens of complex moves that required a cooperative partner. In an effort to create a procedure that should be simple and effective, I discovered a formula, which has since been adopted by military police and military operators. Whether in a confined room or inescapable open space, the knife-disarm rule, or the steps of: 1) grab, 2) close, 3) takedown, 4) escape or counter, are now a defensive standard. The following two scenarios demonstrate this formula in action:

SCENARIO 1

When attacked by a hostile subject with a knife in a confined space, like up against a wall, bring your hands up in order to protect your vital organs.

"Grab" the attacker's weapon hand any way you can because in real combat, there is no "magic grab." Fortunately, this first grab is usually an instinctive move on the part of the defender.

"Close" the distance between you and the attacker by stepping toward him. By jamming him up, you deny the attacker maneuvering room for his weapon.

"Takedown" the attacker whether you get him on the ground or push him off-balance, either way will suffice. Pushes, pulls, trips and sweeps are all acceptable moves.

"Escape" if there is room to get away no matter what because trying to take a knife out of an attacker's hands is often suicidal. Getting away from the scene means you'll have the chance to find a weapon or escape.

"Counter" an attack in situations in which escape is impossible. Remember, this is a deadly force situation in which you must fight by all means necessary to get the knife away from the attacker.

continued on next page

Whether he escapes, counters or takes away the weapon, the operator's primary objective is to put distance between himself and his attacker.

The operator must get to his primary or secondary weapon to follow up with an arrest. Remember that the minimum-reaction distance is 21 feet or seven meters.

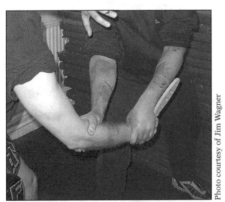

Jim Wagner was one of the first self-defense instructors to introduce stage blood into defensive-tactics training and civilian martial arts.

Another tool Jim Wagner uses is the Canadian-made Shocknife, which delivers up to 7,500 volts when the blade is touched.

Photo courtesy of Jim Wagner

Photo courtesy of Jim Wagner

SCENARIO 2

An attacker armed with a double-edged knife knocks Jim Wagner to the ground. Wagner immediately gets into a side ground-conflict position, which is basically when the operator lies on one side, propped up by one elbow and raises his foot to kick or push away his adversary.

Despite his position, Wagner pushes away his adversary with one foot, but to no avail. As the attacker is determined, Wagner also doesn't have time to ready his weapon.

Because one leg alone will not keep the knife away and help Wagner survive the knife attack, he defends himself with rapid two-feet bicycle kicks.

Once the operator sees an opportunity or a "pause in the conflict," he breaks the attacker's knee with a simple thrust kick. In ground combat like this, do not kick any higher than the knee because no other target will stop the attacker cold.

Breaking the attacker's knee with a firm stomp forces the hostile subject off-balance and gives the operator a better chance to go for a weapon.

In real time, a "pause in conflict" is only a matter of moments, which is why constant practice helps Wagner draw his weapon faster.

continued on next page ▶

Despite his knee injury, the attacker still tries for a final kill. To keep him back, Wagner raises his foot to fend off his determined adversary.

Wagner shoots the center mass, or the area that he can easily target from the ground, which is now the neck area. Note that he must take care not to shoot his own foot in the process. That is why air-gun training is useful reality-based training.

After firing a couple of shots, Wagner gets to his feet, but carefully so as to avoid stumbling. Remember that in reality, the operator could still fall and give his downed attacker a new opportunity to launch an assault, which is why stress practice is a necessity to prepare for these situations.

With the attacker down, Wagner moves back a minimum distance of 21 feet (seven meters) in case his adversary gets up and restarts the attack. Taking cover, if available, is imperative.

משטרת ישראל

Israel Police
Operational Fitness Academy
Havatselet Hasharon
Israel

30.4.01

Re :Sergeant Jim Wagner`s Visit to the Israel
Police Operational Fitness Academy

On behalf of the instructors of the Israel Police
Operational Fitness Academy, I would like to
express our gratitude to Sergeant Jim Wagner for
his visit to our academy last month. His
demonstration and seminar on edged weapons were
very impressive. In the discussion which followed,
we enjoyed the exchange of ideas, which gave us a
new point of view.

We would be very happy to host Sergeant Wagner
again.

Academy Coordinator

Colonel Gidy Lind

Jim Wagner had the opportunity to train the top Israeli municipal and border police defensive-tactics instructors in knife survival. The Israeli air marshals, as well as other units, continue to use some of Wagner's original principles today.

CHAPTER 6

SHIELD DEFENSE

Ballistic shields are used as mobile barricades to make high-risk entries and suspect or vehicle approaches safer. The shield carrier, or "shield man," is usually the point man in these scenarios. He faces unique situations because he must support his shield and weapon at the same time. Moreover, the shield man may need to defend himself against an unarmed attacker, which presents a unique self-defense situation for an operator.

Fortunately, today's shield protection against small-arms fire, fragmentation and hand-thrown debris comes in all shapes and sizes, and they are rated for different caliber impacts. Besides this, ballistics material is also lighter, which means lighter shields are now used in missions, like high-risk car or subject stops (i.e., suicide bombers, narco-terrorism takedowns, gang-member arrests) that didn't use to include the likelihood of a shield attack. For instance, a shield man and his team may need to extract a violent inmate from his cell, but an unarmed attacker may grab his shield or push it into the now-unbalanced operator. A shield attack like this is highly probable in this situation today, which is why operators need to know how to employ their shields offensively as well as defensively.

I started teaching shield-defensive tactics in 1994 when the Los Angeles Housing Authority Police Special Response Team, a unit that did high-risk entries in violent areas on an almost daily basis, asked me to come up with viable shield techniques for their shield operators. While there were plenty of techniques for shooting situations, virtually no tactics were available for shield operators who regularly ran into unarmed aggressors. Almost always, these attackers went for the first person they saw, and that person was the operator holding the shield.

Jim Wagner's students, of the Los Angeles County Sheriff's Department, perform a victim rescue using a ballistic shield for protection.

HOUSING AUTHORITY
POLICE DEPARTMENT
CITY OF LOS ANGELES

CHIEF OF POLICE
ROGER CHANDLER

March 23, 1994

Chief Dave Snowden
Costa Mesa Police Department
99 Fair Dr.
Costa Mesa, Ca., 92626

Dear Sir:

May I take this time to introduce myself to you. I am Lieutenant Piernas with The Los Angeles City Housing Authority Police Department. One of my assignments is Team Leader for our Special Response Team.

As the team leader, I am constantly searching for better training for my officers so they will be better prepared to handle any situation encountered in the field.

It was in this capacity in which I was introduced to one of your officers. Officer Jim Wagner was contacted by one of my officers in reference to providing realistic training for the SRT. Officer Wagner designed several scenarios and provided several people to act as agitators during the training.

This training proved to be very educational and beneficial to the SRT officers. Officer Wagner is an outstanding police officer and trainer. His knowledge and ability to perform as a tactical officer is a credit to his department. It is a privilege to the SRT officers and myself that we can count Officer Wagner as brother in law enforcement.

I would like to thank Officer Wagner for his time, energy, and professional attitude.

Very truly yours,

WILLIE THOMPSON JR.
Acting Chief of Police

R. M. Piernas

ROBERT M. PIERNAS, Lieutenant
SRT Team Leader

515 Columbia Avenue • Los Angeles, California 90017-1295 • (213) 484-0914 • (800) 221-3329 • FAX (213) 484-5395

Jim Wagner received this letter from the Los Angeles Housing Authority Police Special Response Team. This was the first agency that received tactical shield-defense training from him.

SHIELD DEFLECTION AGAINST FRONT KICK

A ballistic shield is a large, inviting target that an unarmed attacker is often tempted to kick. If the operator is not prepared for the impact a solid kick can generate against a shield, he may soon find himself sailing through the air. Here is how to set the attacker off-balance instead:

When approaching an unknown, give him verbal orders to put his hands up and lie facedown on the floor.

Whenever you confront an unknown, be prepared for him to move up to your shield or even kick it. Active resistors often attack shields like bulls charging for red capes. Also, don't forget that unknowns may be concealing weapons.

When the attacker comes in with a forceful kick, bring the shield in tight to your body to prevent secondary impacts. The attacker shouldn't be able to force the shield into your body.

Remember, an unprepared operator who is not well trained in defensive tactics could be sent flying backward or get injured by his own shield.

As the kick comes in, immediately rotate your shield to the side while maintaining a firm grip on the shield handles. Rotate your entire body with the shield, but keep your feet in place.

Deflect the unknown's kick to the side as soon as he makes contact with the shield, thus dissipating the force of the kick as it slides past the shield. Now the unknown is off-balance.

After the deflection, take the attacker down by moving in and pressing him to the floor with the shield. However, if you are with a team, let your teammates flow around the shield and take the attacker down.

These SWAT students use a police car door as a shield while moving up to a target. Such doors are padded with Kevlar and equipped with bulletproof glass.

Photo courtesy of Jim Wagner

SHIELD TILT AND STRIKE

By tilting the shield forward, a shield man can force his attacker to do a leg strike in a very unorthodox manner, which is not pleasant for the kicker. This countering move helps place the top of the shield in position for an impact strike.

An unknown gears up to kick a shield man as his team comes into a room. The alert operator sees the hostile subject's intentions and immediately pulls the shield in tight, bracing for a kick.

This time, the operator doesn't wait to be attacked. Instead, he moves into the unknown to jam him up and prevent his kick from fully developing.

Shoving his shield into the unknown's face, the operator uses the top edge as a striking tool. He shoves hard and presses the shield forward.

If the operator needs to strike the hostile subject a second time because of resistance, he can flip the bottom of the shield upward and shove the edge into his face. This move is also valid if the operator decides to hit the unknown with the top of his shield.

P LITIE

The Head Commissioner of the Policeforce Amsterdam- Amstelland hereby thanks Mr. Jim Wagner for training his instructors on Friday the 18 th may in Amsterdam, together with the instructors of the Royal Dutch Marechaussee.

We thank you for your time and lessons, of which we can profit in the future. We'll hope to see you again soon.

On behalf of the Defence Department,

Amsterdam, 18 th may 2007

Chief inspector Gerard Willemsen
Firearms and Defence Department.

P LITIE

• Regiopolitie Amsterdam Amstelland

Jim Wagner has trained almost every full-time police defensive-tactics instructor in Holland. This includes federal and regional instructors.

SHIELD WALL PIN

Using a shield to pin an out-of-control unarmed inmate to his cellblock wall is a standard world practice in jails and prisons. This same technique is also appropriate for a shield team making entry into a dwelling to press a passive or active unarmed resistor to a wall in order to contain and execute his arrest. In some countries, like the United Kingdom, where most patrol officers do not carry firearms, a shield operator will use this same technique to pin an armed man with a knife while his teammates take the knife from the hostile subject's hand.

A shield man and his teammate confront an unknown, or passive resistor, who does not comply with their lawful orders.

As the operators approach, the unknown turns into an active resistor when he begins to throw arm strikes. The operators are already committed to this conflict and cannot easily move backward.

The operators push forward before the active resistor launches a serious attack. This sudden charge also overwhelms him with what the U.S. Marines call a "violence of action."

The operators pin the unknown between the shield and the wall. As an active resistor, the unknown will inevitably try to grab onto the shield and move it out of his way, but the second operator is ready for this reaction.

The second operator transitions his long gun and moves around the shield to go after the pinned unknown. In the meantime, the shield man will keep applying pressure on the unknown's body.

The shield man's teammate grabs onto the pinned unknown. If the active resistor is still flailing his arms or legs, the second operator will use reasonable force to make him stop by grabbing hold of him at any available point.

The second operator forces the unknown to the ground where both operators can better control him; it also reduces the unknown's chance of possible injuries. During this maneuver, the shield operator covers his teammate.

The second operator makes the arrest, but the shield operator will put down his shield to assist the second operator if called.

The shield operator, if not needed to effect the arrest, covers his partner. If the unknown should pull out a weapon, the shield operator is also close enough to have an accurate shot that will not endanger his teammate.

The arresting operator places the shield on his back so it faces the combat zone's direction and then escorts the unknown out of the area of operations.

CHAPTER 7

ARREST AND CONTROL

If a confrontation ends in favor of the operator, he still must take his adversary into custody, which means he must lay hands on and restrain his downed attacker. This can be a dangerous endeavor because the operator or his team must come in close to a hostile subject who may decide to strike even though the odds are stacked against him. But this leads to an important lesson: In any operation, an operator cannot assume that he has things completely under control, even with an "army" to back him up. Here's a case from my days with the Costa Mesa Police Department to illustrate this point:

Four narcotics officers wanted to stop and search a parolee whom they thought was engaging in criminal activity. A parolee is a convicted criminal who is released from prison before his sentence is up but who agrees to certain conditions in order to obtain his freedom. One of these conditions is that he waives his rights to U.S. search-and-seizure laws, which means the police can search him without probable cause.

Before pulling over the parolee's car and because the narcotics officers were in an unmarked police car, they requested two marked patrol cars to help them make the stop. The two marked units pulled over the parolee and took him out of his car, but the narcotics officers carried out the investigation. While the uniformed patrol officers stood back, one narcotics officer—let's call him Detective A—asked the parolee to comply with a lawful pat-down search by placing his hands on the hood of his car and spreading his legs. The cooperative man replied, "I'll do it, but you won't find anything on me. I'm clean."

Because the parolee was compliant and surrounded by officers—Detective A stood next to him, three narcotics officers stood in a half circle close by and two uniformed officers watched the situation—nobody expected any problems. However, as the parolee turned away from the officers to place his hands on the car's hood, he lifted the front of his shirt and arced around in a smooth, practiced movement while taking out a .45-caliber semiautomatic pistol from his waistband. Without warning, the parolee turned in a full circle to face the officers again, but this time he was visibly armed. He fired at them.

The officers dived for cover, but Detective A was not so lucky. While trying to get to safety, a bullet penetrated his colon and part of his liver. In the end, the parolee was the only fatality, struck down not by the advanced-trained narcotics unit but by the two uniformed patrol officers. Detective A also recovered from his injuries and eventually returned to his duties, but not without having to carry a colostomy bag around for a year.

This story represents the hundreds of similar situations in which operators are attacked during the arrest-and-control phase of a mission when a hostile subject decides to make a last-ditch effort to escape. There are too many dead officers and soldiers who thought they had their prisoners under control only to find out that they were wrong too late. The most important thing to remember when taking a person into custody is that he is always a threat, even with the restraints on, until he is no longer in your care. The second rule to remember is that it's safer not to be the shooter and the arresting officer at the same time because it is not a wise idea to lay hands on a potentially dangerous person with a weapon in hand. When in a team, it is also imperative that an armed partner covers the arresting officer who makes an arrest. That way, if the attacker "gets hinky," or pulls away, the arresting officer can pull back toward safety while his partner meets the attacker with deadly force, if necessary.

Finally, don't tempt a detainee to take your own weapon by not securing it. No matter what unit you are in or how much training you have, a person will always exist who will resist arrest. This is why I devote this chapter to defensive tactics that deal with arrest and control.

In this photo from 2007, Jim Wagner teaches Army National Guard troops U.S. Army Combatives because troops must know the proper use of force for combat and peacekeeping missions.

Photo courtesy of Jim Wagner

ONE-PERSON ARREST AND CONTROL

Although it is always safer to work in teams, real life does not always afford operators that luxury. If circumstances dictate that an operator has to take a person into custody alone, it is imperative for him to know how to control his prisoner safely while putting on the restraints. From my own experience, the second most likely time an arrested enemy decides to fight is when the restraints are being put on him. He knows it is his final chance to escape.

The operator tells an armed adversary with a screwdriver to drop his weapon. For the purposes of this book, the operator's attacker is actually closer than would be acceptable in a real-life situation.

The hostile subject complies with lawful orders, but the operator must consider the possibility of other concealed weapons.

The operator tells his prisoner to raise his hands above his head in order to keep his hands away from his waist area, which is where 90 percent of all weapons are concealed.

The prisoner complies with orders to turn around and keep his hands raised, but the operator is still prepared for a possible attack.

Continuing with the arrest, the operator orders the arrested attacker to interlace his fingers behind his neck. This is the old position used by the Los Angeles Police Department, which I believe is still the best because it keeps a prisoner's hands away from his waist.

The operator squeezes the prisoner's fingers together, making it more difficult for him to pull them apart and suddenly attack. Note that the operator keeps his weapon pulled back and tight to his body.

The operator orders the prisoner down on his knees. If there is going to be a fight, this is usually when it begins. The operator keeps his rifle in close and ready, just in case the prisoner spins around.

When forced to the ground, this prone position makes it harder for the prisoner to get back up, attack and escape.

Placing his knee on the center of the prisoner's back to press him down, the operator pulls up the nearest hand to apply a standard police handcuffing technique.

The operator handcuffs the prisoner's hands. If handcuffs are not practical to carry because of weight, then I recommend nylon restraint devices or zip ties.

PRISONER SEARCH AND MOVEMENT

As a corrections officer, I found many overlooked weapons on inmates and have since learned to take the extra time to search prisoners correctly. After all, a thorough search is a procedure that not only could save an operator's life but also could save the lives of the operators the prisoner is handed over to.

It's a truth that in tactical situations, some operators are sloppy with their searches or just don't have enough time to search the prisoner properly because of a fluid combat situation. If this happens to you, tell the personnel to whom you are releasing your prisoner to search him. Say, "Hey, I only did a cursory pat-down, but you should search this guy again. He might have weapons on him." Remember that searches and movement fall into the category of post-conflict tactics and that they are just as much a part of defensive tactics as actual conflict techniques.

A handcuffed prisoner lies in a prone position for maximum control. If he resists you on the ground, he is probably getting ready to attack, break free and escape.

To begin the weapons search, roll the prisoner onto his side. This is also recommended to prevent restraint positional asphyxiation, a danger for anyone, even healthy individuals, because it restricts the breathing of a person in an already aggravated and tense situation.

Push out the prisoner's top leg and bend it to create a "stand" to stabilize the prisoner's body. Remember to always stay behind the prisoner in a search.

Because 90 percent of all concealed weapons are hidden in the waistband, start the search there. Use a patting technique instead of running your hand up and down the prisoner so as to prevent cutting your hand on "sharps," e.g., needles, knives and edged weapons.

If you find anything in the pockets that could be a weapon, take it out. Because of the possibility of finding sharp objects, you should wear puncture-resistant gloves.

After searching the entire body, sit the prisoner up in order to get him to his feet and transported. For this step and the next, you'll have to assist the prisoner.

To help him up, rotate the prisoner upward by bracing his neck with the nondominant hand while keeping hold of his right upper arm with your dominant one for maximum control.

Tell the prisoner to stand up and then help him to his feet by lifting on his biceps. The cuffed hands help to create a handle for you to lift up.

Once the prisoner is on his feet, diligently anticipate any kicks that could help him break free and run. Remember that just because the prisoner is cuffed does not mean he is helpless.

Escort the prisoner by grabbing the chain of the handcuffs and an arm or the back of his shirt. Remember that even the most secured attacker can still escape, so pay attention and be aware.

BATON STRIKE

Many operators carry impact weapons as a part of their standard-issued equipment. An impact weapon, such as an expandable baton, falls between controlling force on the low end of the use-of-force continuum and deadly force on the high end. In those situations in which less-than-lethal force is required, the operator can only strike "green zone" targets, which only include the limbs. However, if an attacker is about to inflict serious bodily injury or death on an operator who happens to be armed with an impact weapon at the moment, that operator may use his impact weapon as a deadly weapon to strike "red zone" targets, which include the head, neck, torso, pelvic region or any of which can lead to permanent injury or death. Note that striking zones are not to be confused with distance zones (See page 29.) and the two color codes are unrelated.

An unknown subject takes an aggressive posture in front of the operator. The operator gives him verbal orders to sit down, but the hostile subject does not comply.

Recognizing the unknown's aggression, the operator gives him a verbal warning to stop and shows him the international hand signal to stop while displaying his baton.

The operator deploys his expandable baton. Many times, the sound alone of the baton expanding is enough to make many would-be attackers back off because of fear.

Adopting an imminent conflict position, the operator displays the weapon in order to intimidate the unknown. However, this active resistor is determined to attack.

Reasonable force is now justified when the unknown swings his closed fist at the operator.

The operator rightly selects the leg as the target because it is in the "green zone," and he hits with full force in order to stop the unknown's aggression.

Sheriff-Coroner Department

County of Orange, California

This Certifies that

James Wagner

has successfully completed 8 *class hours of instruction in*

Side Handle Baton

and is therefore awarded this

Certificate of Completion

April 9, 1991
Date

Certified Instructor

Brad Gates
Sheriff-Coroner

Jim Wagner's first official baton training class was in 1991. However, Wagner began studying Philippine *kali* with Dan Inosanto in 1977 and was quite adept at using batons by the time he went to the police academy.

CHAPTER 8

ADDITIONAL DRILLS AND EXERCISES

As I have explained in the previous chapters, it is just as important for operators to train in defensive tactics as it is to train in firearms training. In the real world, special-operations operators can no longer rely on the mind-set that their firearms can handle any situation. This is why the additional drills and exercises outlined in this chapter will help strengthen an operator's performance of reality-based techniques through stress conditioning.

Remember that once you've mastered any technique, no matter your skill level, it will only be a question of maintaining that skill by not staying on a plateau. For example, when I was on the Costa Mesa Police Department SWAT team, we had a sergeant who would start every practice by saying, "Today, we are going to go over the basics." This sounded like a good idea for the first few months, but after listening to him say the same thing at each training session for a year, I realized that the sergeant did not know how to take training beyond those basics. As a result, our training sessions were not very challenging or very realistic. Another way to explain this is by using a very important historical story to illustrate my point:

Flavius Josephus was a first-century Jewish general who was captured by the Romans during the first Roman-Jewish War. Given the opportunity to record the Romans' triumph instead of being executed, Josephus recorded that Roman legionnaire training was "a bloodless combat, and their combat [was] bloody training." In other words, Josephus observed no differences between how the Roman's trained and fought; their combat training was as brutal as their actual combat.

Instructors should think: If someone had the opportunity to observe my team's training, like Josephus did with the Roman army, would that observer say that both my training and actual combat experience were one in the same, or would he record that my training only had a few elements that resemble real combat?

The great thing about training today is that we have access to great equipment and innovative gadgets. A good instructor uses these things and sets up realistic scenarios, exercises and drills because his goal is to parallel real life as much as possible. Instructors and operators should use the following drills and this book to spark their imaginations so that they can create training exercises that put stress on students but are also reality-based.

Photo courtesy of Jim Wagner

Before every training session begins, Jim Wagner gives a safety briefing and makes sure all operators have the proper equipment for the training.

Royal   Gendarmerie
Canadian   royale
Mounted   du
Police   Canada

Security Classification/Designation
Classification/désignation sécuritaire

Unclassified

Your File   Votre référence

TO: Jim Wagner

Our File   Notre référence

FROM: Cst Chris St-Jacques
          Prime Minister Protection Detail

SUBJECT: LETTER OF APPRECIATION

On behalf of the Royal Canadian Mounted Police Prime Minister
Protection Detail I would like to thank you for your continuing
contribution in helping to develop our Defensive Tactics program and for
sharing with us the Counter terrorism material obtain during all your
training around the world.

I look forward to a continuing working relationship, and your next visit to
our Capital.

Our best regards

Constable Chris St-Jacques,
Prime Minister Protection Detail

Canada

Jim Wagner has trained dozens of Canadian agencies over the years. In return, he has learned many techniques and tactics, which he incorporates in his courses today.

GUARDING THE BOX

Not all special-operations missions involve moving and shooting hostile subjects because some missions can involve dealing with attackers in a mob. The following training drill is used extensively by bodyguard units around the world and is necessary for all operators to learn when dealing with a group of hostiles or holding a fixed position. The exercise takes place in a box, which represents a fixed post that must be guarded at all costs.

A box of any size is marked on the ground usually in front of a wall or other fixed position. Two or more operators stand inside the box in order to protect it.

Some agitators approach the box, and one has been instructed to penetrate it at any given time. To create a reality-based training exercise, the operators don't know who will carry out the penetration.

The operators sternly order the agitators not to come into the area by using their commanding presence and verbal inflection. At this point, the instructed agitator hasn't made his move, so the operators must be prepared for anything.

As the agitators continue to aggress, the operators remain prepared to repel any type of attack: verbal assault, physical assault and battery or a serious assault like a knife or gun attack.

The man on the right moves up to the edge of the box while verbally assaulting the nearest operator. If the operator believes he is too close, he may take appropriate action to repel him.

The operator decides to use reasonable force and pushes the agitator back before he penetrates the box. He also yells, "Get back! Get back!"

Now, the instructed agitator decides to penetrate the box by taking a swing at one of the operators.

The operator under attack responds with a closed-fist forward strike because he has the legal right to defend himself and his position. The other operator observes because there are multiple opponents and he can't be drawn into the fight unless called in.

If a hostile subject deploys a weapon, even though he may not be penetrating the box, the operators must take the appropriate action using the correct use of force. (See Appendix 1.) In this case, deadly force is required.

MIND OVER PAIN

Sometimes my students call me sadistic because some drills seem more like torture than training. However, every drill and exercise I incorporate into the Reality-Based Personal Protection system is designed to help people survive conflict situations whether they are on battlefields abroad or on the streets of New York City.

In this drill, two students fight over a single weapon or engage in hand-to-hand combat while the instructor waits to shoot one of them with an air or paint gun. During the struggle, the "victim" is too caught up to notice when he will be shot. When it finally happens, the student will feel unexpected pain, but he will have to keep fighting his advancing and uninjured attacker. The idea is that a wound doesn't mean you can quit. This drill will help you both physically and mentally continue to fight.

Jim Wagner, the instructor in this drill, is going to use an AirSoft gun. This training device is also used by police and military units for quick-training scenarios.

He loads the pistol's magazine with 6mm plastic pellets. Paintball guns take a .64-caliber paintball, but they can be messy because of the paint contained inside.

For safety, the two student fighters are outfitted with wraparound eye protection because Wagner will use an AirSoft gun.

The fighters engage in hand-to-hand combat when Wagner gives the command to go. Because of the intensity of the struggle, the fighters easily forget that their instructor will take a shot at them.

As the instructor, Wagner walks around the fighters and looks for a safe place to shoot his targeted trainee. Avoid the groin, neck and ears, as well as any piece of equipment that could mask the pain; the legs, butt or arms are good targets.

The instructor must keep in mind that the fighters can change positions instantly, thus extreme care must be taken to shoot the trainee in the safest manner possible.

When Wagner sees a good spot to target, he fires at close range. Note: A paint gun is stronger than an air gun and can actually injure a trainee unless fired at a farther distance.

After the shot, the trainee continues fighting and doesn't show any pain to his adversary. By doing this, he prevents his attacker from developing a "chase instinct," which occurs when an animal or human sees weakness and takes advantage of it.

After being shot, the trainee's goal is to accept the pain and keep on fighting. When the conflict has ended, he can follow up with self-first aid for added realism.

The instructor is also responsible for making sure that nobody gets hurt by other means, such as through hard takedowns, a trapped arm or leg, or unacceptable roughness. Usually, the instructor will fire one to two shots per person per training exercise.

APPENDICES

Appendix 1
THE USE-OF-FORCE LADDER

Every adversary is going to have the same level of fighting skills and the same reasons for fighting you, right?

Wrong.

Human conflict is unpredictable because there are countless factors involved. Yet with the way most self-defense instructors teach their students how to handle a fight, one would naturally conclude that there is one generic attacker: the worst-case scenario bent on your destruction. Yes, some predators would not hesitate to victimize anyone they cross paths with, but a "cookie-cutter approach" to dealing with conflict can result in personal injury and legal trouble.

Once you actually use your martial arts skills in a real self-defense situation, you will be held legally accountable for your actions. It doesn't matter whether you're a seasoned street cop or you've just completed your third martial arts lesson, some prosecutor or defense attorney is going to bring up the use-of-force issue. They're going to have a field day with you if you can't articulate the different levels of force and what can legally be done at each level. It is therefore imperative that you know what you can and cannot do in any conflict situation.

Based on Standards

As a former soldier, jailer, street cop, SWAT officer, diplomatic bodyguard, counterterrorist with the U.S. government—and now a soldier again teaching combatives—I have had to follow a use-of-force policy. Such a policy protected me if I stayed within its parameters. If, on the other hand, I acted outside the policy guidelines (using unreasonable force or violating someone's constitutional rights), I could have found myself in jail (with criminal charges) or cutting some hefty checks (in a lawsuit).

Ignorance of the law is not a legal excuse that will protect you, especially when it comes to excessive-force cases. Most civilian martial artists have no idea just how much trouble they can get into legally—even when they are in a self-defense situation. A few well-meaning martial artists are sitting in prison right now because they didn't know where to draw the line, or even where the line was to be drawn in the first place.

In the Reality-Based Personal Protection system, the use-of-force ladder is conceptually similar to what the military and civilian law-enforcement agencies must follow.

The Colors of Conflict

Like a real ladder that you would lean up against a building, the most stable place to be is not on the ladder at all. Once you get on the ladder, there are risks. You can get injured from merely a foot off the ground. Similarly, in daily life you are always safest when you avoid conflict; however, trouble can sometimes find you.

Before you go up or down the ladder, you will notice that to the left of the ladder are the subject's actions (your attacker), indicated with a gray triangle, and a vertical arrow next to it with a gradient of colors. The arrow corresponds with the color-coded system:

- Secure (White)
- Caution (Yellow)
- Danger (Orange)
- Conflict (Red)

Secure (White): This level is staying off the ladder altogether and being in a secure place: home, work, social events, etc. Conflict is not anticipated; however, this doesn't mean that you are totally secure. At the white stage (or "code white"), you still must have emergency plans in place. For example, if you are at home, you should have home-security plans: locks, outdoor lighting, alarm system, surveillance cameras, escape routes, etc. Likewise, you must have an escape plan at work should there be a workplace shooting, terrorist attack, etc.

Caution (Yellow): This is the level that you must always maintain when you're in public. Always be aware of your environment: people, vehicles, behind large objects, dark areas, etc. This is not a state of paranoia but rather one of prudent caution known as "situational awareness." That's why the arrow extends below the ladder and into the white area. You should be alert long before you face potential conflict.

Once there is any indication of a conflict, the yellow color blends rapidly into orange. On the ladder, the yellow turns darker when a subject is giving visual indicators such as a hard stare (mad-dogging you), posturing, wearing gang colors, etc.

Danger (Orange): At this level, there is a real possibility of danger because the subject is giving verbal indicators: direct threats, suspicious words, etc. The intensity of this pre-conflict phase can escalate or dissipate. The potential for conflict can be rapid, steady or gradual. Although words themselves cannot hurt you physically, words can determine your course of action. If someone is threatening to hurt you, there must be three elements present before you can take physical action: means, (the wherewithal to harm you), opportunity (the immediate ability to harm you) and intent (the thought to harm you, whether implied [such as a robber with a mask and gun] or verbalized ["I'm going to kill you!"]).

Conflict (Red): At this level, you are in physical conflict. Does this mean you can use whatever self-defense techniques you would like? No. There are many levels of conflict. Even in warfare there are differences: low-intensity conflict (guerrilla warfare, terrorism, etc.) and high-intensity conflict (all-out war or limited actions). A person who pushes you because he is rude should not be treated like someone who is trying to stab you with a knife.

Notice that the left arrow of the graph starts at the bottom of the ladder as a low-risk situation and then escalates to a high-risk situation, and the arrow to the right starts from being cautious to being engaged in physical conflict. The higher you climb any ladder, the more unstable it can become—especially if you are climbing it by yourself. If you are alone when a subject confronts you, you are the only one that can help yourself. If you have other people with you, they can help support you (strength in numbers). Once you go beyond the ladder, you will experience death or injury, just as you would if you had stepped off a real ladder from the top rung (the top of both arrows are black, indicating death or serious injury).

The two arrows in the graph both point upward and downward because a conflict situation may start at any level, at any time. You may find yourself in a code-red situation without going through all of the previous rungs first. For example, if you're standing in a bank and robbers suddenly barge in, blasting away with their guns, you're instantly in the red zone.

In some situations, you may climb the ladder progressively and experience escalation. Other situations may start off in a high state of risk but can present opportunities for de-escalation.

Climbing the Ladder

The Reality-Based Personal Protection Use-of-Force Ladder has four rungs to make use-of-force levels easy to remember. Some cops often complain that their own use-of-force continuum graphs, or "steps" as they are often called, are difficult to remember. You won't have that problem with this one. This ladder will be easy to remember in any conflict situation.

Remember this rule: The suspect's actions will always dictate your actions. A true martial artist stays off the ladder if he or she can help it, but it is a cop or soldier's duty to act if the situation calls for it. That's why when you do come face to face with hostile subjects, you may have no choice but to take some action. As we all know, there are three reactions humans will take in a conflict situation:

1. Flight (get away)
2. Fight (defend yourself)
3. Submit (give into the subject's demands or actions)

Level 1

At level one, a subject or potential attacker uses visual indicators. In other words, you will feel that there is possible danger based on things that you see: a suspicious subject approaching you, somebody who is looking around nervously or a car slowing next to you. No laws are being broken by the subject (as far as you know), but you sense something is wrong, so you prepare yourself mentally for all possibilities.

First, you take on a confident demeanor (as noted under "Your Reaction" in the gray triangle on the right of the chart). This means that you look confident and unafraid. Your facial expressions indicate that you are aware of your environment and you know how to use it to your advantage. Confident demeanor also means that you look like you are either prepared for a direct encounter or you are aware of the danger and you are making a "tactical retreat."

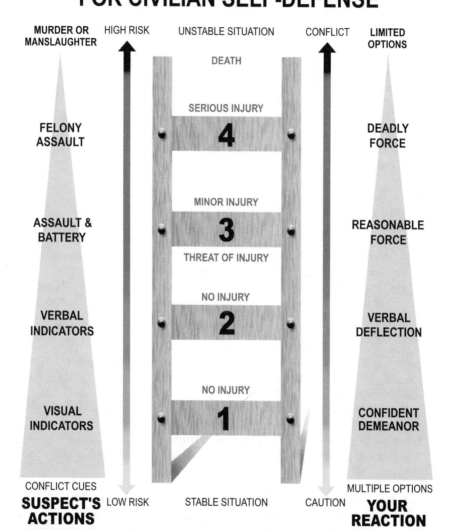

JIM WAGNER REALITY-BASED PERSONAL PROTECTION™

BASED ON THE
UNITED STATES
LEGAL SYSTEM

USE-OF-FORCE LADDER™
FOR CIVILIAN SELF-DEFENSE

SUSPECT'S ACTIONS				YOUR REACTION
MURDER OR MANSLAUGHTER	HIGH RISK	UNSTABLE SITUATION — DEATH	CONFLICT	LIMITED OPTIONS
		SERIOUS INJURY		
FELONY ASSAULT		**4**		DEADLY FORCE
		MINOR INJURY		
ASSAULT & BATTERY		**3** — THREAT OF INJURY		REASONABLE FORCE
		NO INJURY		
VERBAL INDICATORS		**2**		VERBAL DEFLECTION
		NO INJURY		
VISUAL INDICATORS		**1**		CONFIDENT DEMEANOR
CONFLICT CUES	LOW RISK	STABLE SITUATION	CAUTION	MULTIPLE OPTIONS

DEADLY FORCE: Any force that is likely to cause death or serious bodily injury.
REASONABLE FORCE: The level of force that a reasonable person would use in a similar situation.
VERBAL DEFLECTION: Words, or silence, used to diffuse a situation rather than to incite it.
CONFIDENT DEMEANOR: Physical appearance of self-confidence and determination.
THREAT ASSESSMENT: Anticipating likely conflict paths before they occur (at all levels).

Level 2

At the second level, things start to heat up. The subject is actively engaging you or others around you through verbal indicators. This can be anything short of direct threats that warn you an attack is about to happen. Such conflict cues can be anything from the subject's tone of voice to implied threats, or even things you overhear—such as suspicious passengers in an airplane whispering about how "this is going to be a short flight." Those are not alarming words in and of themselves, but some accompanying visual indicators might lead you to suspect a possible terrorist attack.

If a subject is trying to start a fight with you, the best thing to do is to try to calm that person down or ignore him altogether. This is known as verbal deflection. By reacting in this matter, you will not escalate the situation any further. However, in some situations you may have to use a firm, confident voice to talk a subject down. You may have no choice but to try to intimidate him and try to resolve the conflict in this manner. Words will not hurt you physically, but words can be a good indicator of the potential for escalation into physical confrontation.

Level 3

At this point, you enter into physical contact with the subject (or subjects). It may be a precursor push or a punch to the nose—or it could even be a sexual touch (sexual battery). At this level, most martial art instructors teach the cookie-cutter approach. If someone simply pushes you for the sake of intimidation or to get you to swing first, you cannot launch a side kick, blow his knee out and then come crashing down with a drop knee to his spine. If you do, even though you had the right to defend yourself, you would most likely go to jail. This would be "unreasonable force" for the situation.

The conflict at this level can lead to you being injured (a broken nose, cuts, bruises, scrapes, soreness, etc.), but they are neither serious nor life threatening. If a suspect throws a few swings at you, you can't rip his head off. The law won't allow you to do that, even if you did sustain minor injuries from his blows. Because there are no hard-and-fast rules regarding what you can and cannot do in a self-defense situation, the law will judge you by a simple rule: What would a reasonable person do in the same situation?

Assault is the threat of injury. If you feel a threat is visible, you can reasonably defend yourself. Battery is when physical contact is made, be it a push, a punch or someone spitting on you.

Level 4

Near the top of the ladder at the fourth level, serious bodily injury or death is likely to result—whether it's the suspect's, yours or someone you are trying to protect. If a suspect attacks you in a manner likely to result in death or serious bodily injury (felony assault), then you have the right as a citizen to use deadly force. This applies to felony assaults against you and those you choose to protect.

If an attacker is trying to harm someone in your presence, you may (but are not required to) use deadly force. However, if the case goes to court, you will still be judged based on the reasonableness of the force.

Examples of felony assault include attempted murder, mayhem (putting out an eye, severing a limb, ripping off an ear, etc.), rape, caustic chemical attack, robbery, etc. In other words, and remember these words carefully, you must have fear for your life or the life of another.

Notice that the gray triangles start off with broad bases, then taper off to points at the top. The right triangle represents the options you have in a conflict situation. When we start with level one, there are multiple options. You can walk away, call the police, yell for help, etc. However, by the time you are engaged in a life-and-death conflict (level four), there are limited options. If someone is trying to stab you, you have basically one option: control the weapon. If you don't block the knife or grab the hand that controls it, you could end up dead.

Memorize It, Use It

On a real ladder, you do not always have to go up the ladder rung by rung. If you choose to skip a rung, you can. However, by doing so, it is always more unstable. In a real conflict, however, you may have to skip a level. For example, you may have to deal with a man who's wearing a belt bomb (a very real possibility in this day and age). Although no one truly knows the intention of the person (it could be a prank, after all), the "bomb" itself implies intent to blow up himself and anything around him. Therefore, you can go directly from verbal indicator to deadly force, skipping reasonable force altogether based on what you saw.

By memorizing the Use-of-Force Ladder, you and those with whom you train will be able to stay within the law if you ever have to use your self-defense skills. If you're a reality-based instructor, you can start teaching your students the different levels of force and how they can apply the appropriate techniques to each level. By doing this, you teach them two important things:

1. There is no such thing as a generic attacker.

2. How to survive the justice system when they use the techniques you have taught them.

Photo courtesy of Jim Wagner

Jim Wagner and a training partner stand in front of an aircraft during Federal Air Marshal School.

Appendix 2

GROUND SURVIVAL

The ground is the last place you want to be during a fist or knife fight because you give up mobility, visibility and the option of being on the offense. On the other hand, if someone is shooting at you, the ground can be used to your tactical advantage.

My Ground Survival course, which is part of the Reality-Based Personal Protection system, focuses on modern tactics, such as how to hit the deck when you're under gunfire, military-style ground movement, using the ground as an impact weapon, subject takedowns and tackle defense. Participants will learn about ambush survival, perceptual distortion during a conflict and other reality-based concepts. The hands-on training includes multiple-attacker situations, escape techniques and less-than-ideal conflict positions. To learn more about the Ground Survival course, visit: www.jimwagnertraining.com.

Photo courtesy of Jim Wagner

Jim Wagner is on bicycle patrol in 1997 while serving on the Costa Mesa Police Department. In some tactical situations, bicycles can be a nice, fast, silent way to sneak up on a target.

Appendix 3

HAND-GRENADE ATTACKS

During my time as a sergeant at the Orange County Sheriff's Department in Southern California, our bomb squad received about 500 calls a year to handle explosive devices. Many of those calls were for hand-thrown devices.

Although training for a grenade attack may seem a little too "far-fetched" for many martial artists to waste any valuable time on, keep in mind that these attacks do occur from time to time. The most infamous event that comes to mind is the Columbine High School massacre, which took place April 20, 1999, in suburban Denver. Not only did the two shooters (students Eric Harris and Dylan Klebold) go around shooting fellow classmates and teachers with firearms, but they also were armed with "homemade grenades," the London Free Press reported.

It doesn't take much to make a pipe bomb. For years, this information was accessible on the Internet under the subject "bombs." Countless books on the subject still circulate in used bookstores and at garage sales. Of course, a terrorist needs only to lay down $100 or less to buy an Eastern European fragmentation grenade on the black market.

Without military training, most people have no idea how to defend against a grenade or improvised explosive device (IED) attack. Sadly, most police officers don't even know how to. Such training is usually reserved for SWAT officers. However, this is a survival skill that everyone in today's society should know, and that's why I teach it to the public.

Let's say that you're at the ticket counter of the airport waiting in line between the ropes. Suddenly, you hear the "Tink! Tink! Tink!" of a metal ball bouncing on the hard waxed tile floor behind you. You look and see that it is a drab olive grenade that's missing its "spoon" (the last safety device of the grenade). What should you do?

I can tell you what 99 percent of the public would do: They would get blown to pieces. Here is what YOU should do:

1. Observe where the grenade lands. Not only should you note where the grenade lands but also where it might roll. Most grenades are round and can roll quite a ways from where they first hit the ground. If it rolls in your direction, your chances of survival diminish.

2. Dive away and go facedown. Do not run from a grenade, which has just landed, because you don't know when it will explode. You may be struck with fragments (shrapnel) while trying to flee or get spun in the air by the shock front. Although a grenade has a timer fuse, there is no telling when it will go off. Some fuses are designed to go off in two seconds, while others go off in five seconds. If the thrower wants to take no chances of someone picking up the grenade to throw it back or to throw it into a safe area, he does a technique called "cooking." He releases the spoon ("pulls the pin"), lets the grenade cook off for a second or two and then throws it. This technique allows the grenade to burst in the air or explode on immediate contact with the ground, giving the victims no chance to react.

3. Point your legs toward the grenade and bring your heels together. Your legs should be like an arrow pointing to the grenade, and your feet are the arrowhead. By placing the soles of your shoes together, they act like a shield between the rest of your body and the device. If shrapnel does come your way, hopefully your shoes, feet and legs will absorb it before it penetrates vital organs.

4. Bring your elbows to the side of your rib cage and cover your ears with your hands. By using your arms to cover your torso and your hands to cover your head, you are using your limbs as a buffer between flying debris and vital areas of your body.

5. Close your eyes and open your mouth. When a grenade explodes, a shock front (also known as a "shockwave") expands outward from the center. This sudden high-pressure area moving through the atmosphere can rupture your eardrums and your lungs if you are close enough (it takes only 80 pounds per square inch to rupture the lungs). By keeping your mouth open, you are attempting to equalize the outside pressure with your internal air cavities to avoid a rupture.

Photo courtesy of Jim Wagner

Jim Wagner emerges from the water during a tactical swimmer course taught by U.S. Marine personnel. Wagner trained for several years in Maritime Interdiction in Los Angeles and Miami.

BLACK BELT.
P R E S E N T S

JIM WAGNER'S
REALITY-BASED PERSONAL PROTECTION
DVD SERIES

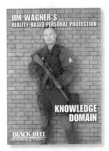

KNOWLEDGE DOMAIN

Jim Wagner introduced the term "reality-based" to the martial arts world through *Black Belt* magazine in 1998. *Knowledge Domain* is everything you need to know about reality-based personal protection. As one New York instructor put it, "This is the 'missing link' of the martial arts." Concepts include the Jim Wagner Use-of-Force Ladder, the OODA process, training-environment control and conflict rehearsal. (Approx. 61 min.)

DVD Code 9109—Retail $29.95

DEFENSIVE TACTICS

Defensive Tactics is based on easy-to-learn modern military and police techniques and training methods. This step-by-step program demonstrates threat zones, conflict stances, movements and arm strikes using the Jim Wagner piston concept. Other topics include stopping power, arm blocks using the angle principle, effective leg strikes and counters, and ways to properly execute the head butt. Legal issues dealing with the use of force are also discussed. (Approx. 49 min.)

DVD Code 9119—Retail $29.95

GROUND SURVIVAL

Should you end up on the ground, *Ground Survival* will teach you how to use this otherwise undesirable position to your tactical advantage. Topics include the best method for hitting the deck, subject takedowns, tackle defense, the ground-conflict position and ways to generate powerful arm strikes from the ground. Learn the latest police and military recovery methods for escape and evasion, how to use the environment to your advantage and how to get back on your feet. (Approx. 56 min.)

DVD Code 9129—Retail $29.95

KNIFE SURVIVAL

The knife is the most common weapon used by criminals and terrorists, with the average knife attack lasting a mere five seconds. *Knife Survival* will take you step by step through the 12 angles of attack, the four primary blocks, the proper grip and the Jim Wagner knife-disarm rule. Includes proven conflict drills designed to increase your speed and reaction time: the feeding drill, the one-for-one drill and the freestyle drill. (Approx. 58 min.)

DVD Code 9139—Retail $29.95

Notes:

Notes:

Notes:

Notes: